VERBAL BEHAVIOR
Adaptation and Psychopathology

Walter Weintraub, M.D.

SPRINGER PUBLISHING COMPANY
New York

To Monique

Copyright © 1981 by Springer Publishing Company, Inc.

Springer Publishing Company, Inc.
200 Park Avenue South
New York, New York 10003

81 82 83 84 85 / 10 9 8 7 6 5 4 3 2 1

Library of Congress Cataloging in Publication Data

Weintraub, Walter
    Verbal behavior.

    Includes bibliographical references and index.
    1. Verbal behavior. 2. Psycholinguistics.
3. Personality. 4. Personality assessment. 5. Mental
illness—Diagnosis. I. Title. [DNLM: 1. Verbal behavior.
2. Psychopathology. 3. Defense mechanisms. WM 100
W426v]
BF455.W37   153.6   80-27021
ISBN 0-8261-2660-X
ISBN 0-8261-2661-8 (pbk.)

Printed in the United States of America

Contents

Preface

During the summer of 1959, while vacationing with my family on Martha's Vineyard, I amused myself for about an hour each day recording spontaneous remarks made by my three oldest children. At the time, I was preoccupied with the problem of identifying manifestations of psychological coping mechanisms in speech, and I believed that the naive, unsophisticated language of children was ideally suited for such an investigation. I made it my practice to write down comments made during periods of stress and conflict, such as might follow denied requests, punishments, sibling arguments, and so on. Philippe, Eric, and Michèle, aged eight, five, and three, respectively, were the innocent and unconsenting subjects for my informal study. At the time, my wife, Monique, was visibly pregnant with Danny, our youngest child. Although unable to participate actively in the experiment, Danny served as a useful stimulus for some of his sister's most interesting remarks.

When we returned to Baltimore after our vacation, I lost interest in the study and filed away with other uncompleted projects the notebook containing my children's comments. Last Christmas, when the children returned home from college and professional school for the holidays, Michèle, a 20-year-old junior at Stanford, discovered the notebook while rummaging through the attic. She spent an entire afternoon reading the material and emerged from the experience visibly shaken. "You know," she said, "I still talk the way I did when I was three years old. Is it possible that I haven't changed in 17 years?" Michèle showed the notebook to her two older brothers. They were equally fascinated by the contents and quickly recognized their verbal styles.

In a way, my uncompleted project was brought to an end in a most unexpected and felicitous manner. In a natural and spontaneous way, my children demonstrated that the way we speak under stress is characteristic, that verbal defenses are molded very early in life, and that the grammatical structures associated with verbal style have an extremely slow rate of change.

My interest in speech as a reflection of behavior was stimulated by Dr. Jacob Finesinger, my first psychotherapy supervisor. When I met him in 1956, Dr. Finesinger was Chairman of the Department of Psychiatry at the University of Maryland School of Medicine. I was then a first year resident in psychiatry at the Veterans' Administration Hospital at Perry Point, Maryland, where Dr. Finesinger consulted one afternoon a week. "Jake," as we all called him, was one of the first psychiatrists to use electronically recorded interviews in his supervision. He taught his students that syntax and paralanguage were no less important than meaning in the understanding of the psychotherapeutic process. Jake believed that the future of psychotherapy research lay in the microscopic analysis of small samples of recorded speech.

In 1957 I began formal psychoanalytic training at the Baltimore Psychoanalytic Institute. I was surprised to discover the extent to which experienced analysts rely upon the syntactic and paralinguistic aspects of speech in assessing levels of resistance in their patients' associations. This facet of the analyst's art is represented hardly at all in the voluminous literature on psychoanalytic technique and is largely unappreciated outside the analytic community.

Although clinicians like Lorenz and Jaffe had written extensively about the defensive uses of grammatical structures, no systematic attempts had been made to categorize these speech habits and to relate them to nonverbal behavior. When I joined the faculty of the University of Maryland in 1957 as a research associate, I began to study the speech patterns of groups of individuals sharing styles of deviant behavior. A psychologist colleague in the Department of Psychiatry, Dr. Harriet Aronson, collaborated with me for about 10 years. Together, we developed methods of data collection and analysis and completed a number of studies relating verbal mannerisms to forms of psychopathology.

Following Dr. Aronson's departure from the University of Maryland, I continued to apply the methods we had developed to a variety of clinical areas. These included the expression of psychological defense mechanisms in the speech of children and adolescents, the reflections of adaptation in free writing, and the speech pattern associated with explosive anger.

The publication of the Watergate Transcripts offered me an opportunity to apply verbal behavior analysis to certain psychohistorical problems. I had long been dissatisfied with the traditional methods of psychoanalytic biographers who attempt elaborate psychodynamic and psychogenetic reconstructions of historical figures on the basis of selected incidents in the lives of their chosen subjects. It seemed to me that the systematic scrutiny of free speech and free writing might offer the psychohistorian a new source of reliable data from which inferences about historical figures could be made.

Of the studies to be described in this book, only certain data related to deviant behavior have been published previously. From the beginning, I have found psychoanalytic theory to be the most useful frame of reference for the ordering of my data. More recently, I have been impressed by the possibility that transformational grammar may have a role to play in the generation of new hypotheses. An attempt to look at verbal defense from the point of view of transformational grammar will be made in the concluding chapter.

Acknowledgments

Verbal behavior research is slow, tedious work. Of the many individuals who have helped in the collection and scoring of data, I wish to thank Dr. George Sjolund, Dr. Philip Lavine, Dr. John Carrill, and Dr. Anna Klumpp.

Dr. S. Michael Plaut has been extremely useful in advising me on all phases of the preparation of the manuscript. Without his generous contribution, my task would have been infinitely more difficult.

Finally, I wish to acknowledge the help of Dr. Herbert Gross, a fellow investigator of verbal behavior at the University of Maryland School of Medicine. Dr. Gross' thoughtful comments have been particularly useful in the interpretation of data relating to the verbal expressions of emotion.

Chapter 1
Clinical Communication

As students of behavior, we are interested in the various ways people express their needs and desires. Much of what constitutes clinical wisdom in psychiatry is the ability, acquired over many years of training and practice, to perceive and interpret expressions of thought and feeling. During the past 30 years, remarkable technological progress in the transmission, recording, and interpretation of human messages has enabled us to begin to test in the laboratory hypotheses generated in more natural environments by psychoanalysts, anthropologists, linguists, and ethnologists.

In a general way, clinical communication is concerned with the planning, encoding, transmission, reception, and interpretation of patients' messages. Although these messages may contain data of various kinds, they always provide us with information about the patient. It does not follow, however, that intent always can be inferred from the effect of a message. We should not assume, for example, that a tedious, obsessional individual consciously or unconsciously wishes to bore his listener or that a schizophrenic person desires to perplex those around her. We recognize, of course, that such an assumption often is useful in the conduct of psychoanalytic psychotherapy.

Normal Variations in Human Communication

Any or all aspects of the communication process, that is, the planning, encoding, transmission, reception, and interpretation of messages, may be disturbed. Since, as clinicians, we are interested primarily in pathological deviations as they affect individual patients, we must be aware of the major sources of normal variations in the populations we serve. Many years ago, the American linguist, Edward Sapir (1927), pointed out that each society limits its members to a certain range of intonation of voice, to specific speech rhythms, and to particular ways of pronouncing words. Social and cultural forces, however, do much more than influence voice quality and vocal dynamics. They determine which of our desires are encoded into messages, the verbal and nonverbal behaviors by which they are transmitted, the manner in which they are perceived, and the meaning that we derive from them.

Cultural Influences

To what extent are transcultural similarities in expressive sounds and movements influenced by hereditary factors? Ethnologists and anthropologists have not yet reached a consensus on this question. It is well known that Charles Darwin (1955) believed in the biological transmission of certain expressive gestures in humans. He was convinced by certain observations that even nonhuman primates show sadness and fear in ways similar to those of humans. More recently, other investigators have published data suggesting that some human movements, such as raising the eyebrows and sagging the shoulders, have similar meaning across cultures. Inborn patterns of facial expression appear to be shown by congenitally blind and deaf children. They cough, cry, and show surprise much like other children (Eibl-Eibesfeldt, 1974).

Nativist views have been discounted by anthropologists who believe that culture alone determines the form and content of human messages (Birdwhistell, 1974). Even those who reject an extreme environmentalist position agree that important differences in communication style are associated with culture and national origin. Significant variations among individuals can be traced easily to regional and class differences within a country. In a given city, we can often identify people with specific neighborhoods on the basis of their styles of verbal and nonverbal behavior.

Sexual Variations

Investigators recently have identified a number of differences in the way men and women transmit and receive messages. There is some evidence to support the popular prejudice that women are more competent than men in both expressing and perceiving emotions. In a recent study, for example, female college student pairs were reported to be more successful than male pairs in transmitting and receiving nonverbal emotional cues (Buck et al., 1972). The authors attributed this superiority "to a more overt and 'readable' nonverbal signal from the female senders or to a heightened sensitivity to nonverbal cues by the female observers or both."

Compared to men, women have been reported to make more direct eye contact in one-to-one encounters (Watson, 1972) and to make greater use of the intimate side-by-side sitting position (Sommer, 1959). Birdwhistell (1974) has argued that since many sexual differences in communication are not found among small children and the elderly, they may be determined and maintained largely by cultural forces. In assessing gender display in a number of cultures, he reported, "Informants from all these societies either volunteered or without hesitation responded that young children matured into these behaviors and that as people got older they gave up or matured out of them." Biologically oriented investigators might counter with the claim that Birdwhistell's observations also could be explained by age-related endocrine changes.

Buck has been unable to demonstrate in preschool children sexual differences in the ability to send nonverbal emotional stimuli similar to those he and his colleagues reported for adult subjects (Weitz, 1974, p. 15). He speculated that socialization pressures for male inhibition of emotional expression may not become effective until later in the life of the child.

Age

We do not yet have definitive data relating to the communication patterns of individuals of different ages. Most careful developmental studies have been carried out with very small children. Adolescents and adults have been ignored almost completely. Investigators apparently have assumed that changes in communication style among older subjects either are too small to warrant systematic study or are unimportant for the understanding of language and speech development. In Chapter 3, we shall show that much of value can be learned from a close scrutiny of the verbal performance of individuals of all ages.

Socioeconomic Background

We owe to Basil Bernstein and his associates the development of a sociolinguistic perspective in verbal behavior research. Bernstein (1959, 1960) has demonstrated significant grammatical and paralinguistic differences between middle-class and working-class British children, variations he has attributed to different styles of child rearing. Similar positive associations have been reported between syntactical maturity and level of education (Hunt, 1970; Loban, 1963).

Social Distance

The greater the degree of familiarity, the more accurate the transmission and reception of messages appears to be. Weitz (1974) referred to Dittman's belief that channels of communication change as a function of the depth of a social relationship. As people get to know each other better, "they use more subtle gradations of expressions and rely more on subcultural variations common to both or decoded by each member" (p. 16). The use of indigenous paraprofessionals in community mental health centers is a clinical application of this concept.

Power Relationships

The weaker and more dependent member of a dyad seems to be more perceptive than the stronger member. Clinical observations and laboratory data suggest that women, children, and members of minority groups are extremely sensitive to the moods and attitudes of the more powerful people around them. The doctor–patient relationship is an excellent example of how the stimulation of dependent urges can sharpen the perceptive powers of the weaker member of a dyad. Patients in psychoanalysis quickly become attuned to a variety of nuances in the analyst's voice. In one study, a doctor's success in referring alcoholics for additional treatment was related to the degree of anxiety perceived in his voice (Milmoe et al., 1967).

Number of Receivers

Whether we communicate with one, two, or more individuals affects the way we plan, encode, transmit, and receive messages. Certain people who speak quite articulately in small groups show signs of syntactic disorganization when addressing large audiences. Some stutterers suffer from the opposite difficulty. Although their ability to speak in dyadic or small-group situations may be almost paralyzed, they can talk fluently into a microphone before large groups.

Affective States

Our emotions undoubtedly influence the form as well as the content of our communications. Anxiety, anger, sadness, and elation influence our gait, posture, gestures, voice, and language. Most researchers believe that vocal dynamics are more powerful conveyers of emotions than the verbal content of spoken messages. Some supporting evidence for this position comes from reports indicating that little communication of affect is lost when spoken messages are filtered of their verbal content (Davitz & Davitz, 1959).

Pharmacological Agents

Modifications of speech patterns have been reported in association with the ingestion of alcohol, barbiturates, hallucinogens, marijuana, and other drugs. In one published study, a decrease in the variety of spoken words under the influence of chlorpromazine and amobarbital was found (Fink, Jaffe, & Kahn, 1960). Changes in formal characteristics of speech also have been reported following electroconvulsive therapy. The alterations observed were in the direction of greater use of denial, qualification, displacement, and evasion (Kahn & Fink, 1958).

The list just given does not exhaust the number of variables that may influence the form and content of normal communication. Indeed, one of the difficulties in conducting careful research in the area of clinical communication is the impossibility of taking into account all possible significant factors. As Lorenz & Cobb (1952) have commented, "The concept of a 'control' group cannot be maintained when there are infinite variables."

Pathological Communication

We have learned from Freud that a great deal of disordered communication occurs among otherwise normal people. Occasional slips of the tongue and pen, blocking, stammering, forgetting, mishearing, and misreading are all part of the "psychopathology of everyday life" (Freud, 1966). When our communication becomes so disturbed that we cannot express our needs in a clear, consistent way, the existence of psychiatric illness usually can be inferred.

Can communication be severely disordered in the absence of emotional illness? We are faced with two conflicting points of view. Certain clinicians believe that a great deal of what we call "psychopathology" is nothing more than disturbed patterns of verbal and nonverbal behavior acquired during childhood in conflict-ridden families. For proponents of this view, treatment consists of the active identification and correction of self-defeating styles of communication. Other clinicians believe that persistent functional disorders of speech and movement are symptomatic of underlying psychiatric illness and are more apt to favor psychoanalytic psychotherapy. In the latter form of treatment, therapists deal with communication difficulties as resistances to the uncovering of the unconscious conflicts believed to be responsible for their origin and maintenance.

The Monitoring System in Human Communication

Researchers have focused their attention increasingly upon the functioning of a monitoring system that screens and processes the stream of intrapsychic and interpersonal messages. We select from this stream certain stimuli for attention, reject others, and under normal conditions maintain a harmonious balance between externally and internally derived information. One of Freud's greatest achievements was to demonstrate that most of our monitoring occurs out of awareness and is at least in part regulated by the wish to obtain the maximum degree of pleasure permitted by external reality and the demands of conscience.

Psychoanalytic observers have described in great detail many of the ways in which patients repress, deny, and distort messages that threaten to become sources of intrapsychic conflict. Recently, investigators working in communications laboratories have begun to study some of the ways in which we monitor interpersonal messages. In the course of development, we learn automatically to assess and control the impact of our messages on others. This monitoring is far from perfect. In our nonverbal communication, our faces and hands are less likely to betray us than our legs and feet (Ekman & Friesen, 1969). As a general rule, the greater the degree of intrapsychic conflict, the more likely will interpersonal communication be subject to pathological distortion.

The form and content of the messages we transmit are determined in part by signals emitted by our receivers. There is laboratory evidence to indicate that a listener's movements may be coordinated with the speaker's flow of speech. At times these movements actually may mirror those of the speaker, a possible indication of good rapport. A listener's movements are an important source of feedback for the speaker. A listener who is "in tune" with the speaker will anticipate what is about to be said, make appropriate gestures and sounds, and thus facilitate the flow of conversation (Kendon, 1970).

In summary, our monitoring system screens and processes messages impinging upon us from both external and internal sources. The level of intrapsychic conflict is controlled by directing attention away from disturbing messages or by distorting their meaning. Under normal conditions, we maintain an optimum degree of informational flow from the environment by preventing the dangers of sensory overload and deprivation. Interpersonal conflict is minimized by the careful scrutiny of transmitted messages; this task is assisted greatly by signals from the receiver.

Categories of Data in
Clinical Communication

Clinicians have been systematically observing and describing the behavior of their patients for thousands of years. Although much useful information has been accumulated and transmitted from one generation of investigators to the next, it has been, of necessity, anecdotal. With the development of sophisticated sound and visual recording devices, we now can obtain permanent and faithful records of patients' verbal and nonverbal behavior.

What kinds of observations constitute the legitimate subject matter of clinical communication? There are eight major categories of clinical messages, which may be divided conveniently into spoken and nonspoken behavior.

Spoken Behavior

Paralanguage. Researchers interested in paralinguistics are concerned with the nonverbal aspects of speech. Included in this category are such variables as voice quality, intonation, pitch, volume, and rhythm. Most paralinguists believe that the communication of affect is primarily by means of nonverbal channels of speech (Davitz & Davitz, 1959; Starkweather, 1956). Paralinguistic variables also have proved to be useful in the study of personality traits and interactional states.

Verbal behavior. In this category, we include both the lexical meaning of the message and its syntax or style. Syntactical variables usually can be defined with a degree of precision that allows for more objective scoring than is possible with categories based upon thematic aspects of speech. Investigators interested in semantic variables often are concerned with psychological conflict and motivation; students of verbal style are more apt to be preoccupied with personality traits. Both approaches have been used to monitor transient, affective states.

Nonspoken Behavior

Body language. Gait, posture, gestures, and facial expressions are all excellent transmitters of both intended and unintended messages. As in the case of spoken behavior, we must be familiar with regional and ethnic variations before translating nonverbal messages/ In recent years, the practice of wildly interpreting body language has developed into a kind of parlor game similar to the unsolicited analysis of slips of the tongue in the early days of psychoanalysis. Body language, like other forms of communication, always must be judged in the total clinical context in which it is observed./ Advances in cinematic and television technology have made the careful recording and systematic analysis of body language possible in a variety of settings. Cross-sectional and longitudinal studies that tap transcultural, regional, and individual variations have been completed (Davis, 1972).

Writing. Although usually neglected in diagnosis and treatment, patients' written productions, in the form of diaries, letters, and suicide notes, are rich sources of clinical data. Compared to the amount of investigative work done with speech, researchers have done relatively little analysis of patients' writing. We do not know yet how personality is expressed in writing or what the relationship may be between free speech and free writing. As in the case of spoken language, we must distinguish the verbal content of writing, with its semantic and syntactic variables, from the various nonverbal or calligraphic elements.

Spatial behavior. The ways in which we use space have great psychological significance. Astute clinicians always have noted where patients choose to sit, how they position themselves with respect to the therapist, and how much of the office space they control during a diagnostic or therapeutic session. Family and group psychotherapists are particularly sensitive to seating arrangements and may try to manipulate spatial behavior as a strategy of treatment.

The study of spatial behavior in different cultures has been pioneered by an anthropologist, Edward T. Hall (1966). Other investigators have explored the psychological significance of the use of space. In a study of the connection between spatial arrangement and group task, Sommer (1965) found, for example, that cooperating pairs sat side-by-side, conversing pairs diagonally, and competing pairs opposite from one another.

Clothing and ornamental wear. This channel of communication is extremely informative and always is attended to by conscientious clinicians. The care with which clothes and ornaments are worn, the vividness of color, and the congruence with current fashion are a few of many factors that inform us about patients' moods and personality traits. Depressed patients characteristically wear dark clothes. A touch of bright red in an otherwise somber clothing ensemble should alert us to the possibility of manic potential in a depressed patient. Obsessional people usually dress meticulously and conservatively; seductive, hystrionic individuals often wear attention-stimulating, provocative clothing.

We may include in this category hair styles, mustaches, beards, makeup, and perfumes. Like other channels of communication, clothing and ornamental wear can be interpreted only in the total context of the patient's verbal and nonverbal behavior. Familiarity with current styles and the customs of the social group to which the patient belongs will prevent us from making unwarranted inferences.

Autonomic-nervous-system responses. These reactions often reveal to us otherwise-hidden affective states and should be monitored carefully. Astute clinicians always look for evidence of blushing, tearing, sweating, and pallor and listen for gastrointestinal and respiratory sounds. Extremely interesting studies correlating patterns of verbal behavior with changes in psychophysiological states have been published. In one such study, levels of outwardly directed hostility, estimated from the manifest content of speech samples, correlated significantly with increases in diastolic blood pressure in women with essential hypertension (Gottschalk, 1973).

Observer's responses to patients' behavior. Information of great diagnostic importance can be gathered by the disciplined clinician who is trained to monitor her or his internal responses to patients' behavior. These internal messages may take the form of thoughts, feelings, autonomic responses, and so forth. A feeling of fatigue, for example, may be a message to the therapist that he or she is in a one-sided giving relationship with a passive, dependent patient. Controlling, obsessional patients not infrequently elicit feelings of frustration and anger in their therapists. The alert clinician continuously samples these internal reactions and uses the data to gain further understanding of the clinical situation.

The psychoanalytic literature contains a great deal of anecdotal information on therapists' reactions to patients. Attempts have been made to observe reactions to patients' behavior in more systematic ways. In a study recently published (Coyne, 1976), it was found that normal subjects who had conversed on the telephone with depressed patients became significantly more despondent, anxious, hostile, and rejecting themselves. This response did not occur after they spoke to nondepressed volunteers. The author concluded that this "environmental response may play an important role in the maintenance of depressed behavior."

Verbal Style in Clinical Communication

In the succeeding chapters, we shall be concerned almost entirely with style in verbal behavior. By means of a series of clinical studies, we shall demonstrate that the investigation of syntactical, nonsemantic aspects of speech is an objective and fruitful approach to the study of personality.

We do not claim that attention to style is superior to other strategies of psycholinguistic research. Certain investigators tend to emphasize the importance of their work by claiming a special priority for a particular channel of communication. Paralinguists, for example, usually contend that vocal dynamics is the royal road to the understanding of affective states, since naive observers appear to rely most upon this mode of transmission. We must distinguish, however, between the perceptions of untrained observers and sophisticated ones. In Chapter 7, we shall show that explosive anger is associated with a pattern of verbal behavior that can be traced solely from typed transcripts of free speech samples. Investigators interested in developing methods of detecting and measuring affective states need not limit themselves to the ways in which emotions normally are transmitted and received. In the long run, we must judge the usefulness of a procedure by its convenience, accuracy, economy, and range of applicability.

To a much greater extent than is generally realized, sophisticated psychoanalytic clinicians depend upon syntactic cues in their assessment of psychological conflict and patterns of defense. Experienced therapists often will dismiss as insincere "insightful" comments by patients largely on the basis of vocal and syntactical criteria. Much of this clinical wisdom has not appeared in the literature because the psychoanalytic tradition emphasizes the primacy of thematic content and the intuitive assessment of intent.

We believe that the present disorganized state of verbal-behavior research stems partly from the failure of any one system to win over large numbers of adherents. Few studies have been replicated, and terms are defined in different ways by different investigators, making comparisons of results almost impossible. In the words of one critic, "Dozens of content-analysis systems have been developed for the study of counseling or therapeutic interviews. With few exceptions, such systems have been used in only one or two studies, usually by the authors, and then have passed into obscurity" (O'Dell & Winder, 1975). Systems of verbal behavior analysis require greater simplicity, economy, and precision before we can expect more widespread, consistent use.

Assumptions and Strategies

Our approach to verbal behavior research has been guided by three assumptions: (1) patterns of thinking and behaving are reflected in styles of speaking; (2) under stress, a speaker's choice of syntactic structures will mirror characteristic coping or defense mechanisms, and (3) personality traits are revealed by grammatical forms having a slow rate of change.

We do not know how differences in the choice of syntactic structures develop. As in the case of other ego functions, hereditary and early familial influences probably play a crucial role. Systematic differences in the choice of grammatical forms have been reported among children under the age of two (Nelson, 1977a).

Some Previous Attempts to Correlate Speech and Personality

Our efforts to relate formal characteristics of speech to personality variables continues a tradition of clinical research that began about 50 years ago.

In an early study, Busemann (1925) recorded in shorthand a number of stories told by children of different ages on such subjects as "An Outing," "A Christmas Celebration," and the like, and then divided the number of verbs by the number of descriptive words. This ratio, which he called the "Action Quotient," increases with the relative increase in the number of verbs and decreases with the relative increase of adjectives. Busemann reported that the Action Quotient fluctuated rhythmically with age and reflected variations of emotional stability and creative power. With certain modifications, Busemann's Action Quotient was applied by Boder (1940) to written material of various kinds. He found that the ratio of adjectives to verbs increased as he proceeded from plays to legal statutes to fiction to scientific monographs.

In an attempt to study objectively the psychodynamics of different neurotic syndromes, Balkan & Masserman (1940) analyzed the fantasies of patients diagnosed as "obsessional," "conversion hysteric," and "anxiety state." Formal, grammatical criteria were used. The authors reported, among other findings, that obsessional patients qualified most and reported the longest fantasies; conversion hysterics had a low verb–adjective quotient and showed little vagueness or qualification; the fantasies of anxiety hysterics, on the other hand, were characterized by brevity and a high verb–adjective quotient.

Some of the most detailed reports of the speech patterns of psychiatric populations were published by Maria Lorenz (1955), who identified many verbal mannerisms associated with deviant personality traits. Her descriptions of patients' verbal behavior were unusually sensitive and persuasive.

Another influential investigator in the field of verbal behavior is Joseph Jaffe. Imaginative and versatile, he has made a number of conceptual and technical contributions. Although his most careful investigations have been in the area of paralanguage, Jaffe has made important observations related to verbal style. A practicing psychoanalyst, he was one of the first to realize that his analyst colleagues do in fact "attend to the formal aspects of communication as much as to the content [but that] they are often unaware of the precise nature of the cues which are the bases of their clinical impressions" (Jaffe, 1961). Among Jaffe's many contributions to the psychology of speech have been the application of Ruesch & Bateson's analysis of communication networks to clinical practice, the use of precise nonverbal measures to study dyadic communication, and the application of computer technology to the processing of clinical messages. With respect to verbal style, Jaffe, like Lorenz, identified many of the speech habits by which patients in psychoanalysis reveal their personality traits and noted that certain diagnostic categories are associated with the use of specific verbal mannerisms (Jaffe, 1960a).

A major contributor to the field of verbal behavior is Louis Gottschalk, a trained psychoanalyst familiar with both clinical and laboratory procedures. Gottschalk's proclaimed goal is "to probe the immediate emotional reactions of subjects or patients, instead of the typical or habitual ones" (1973). In his view, studying emotional reactions through the analysis of verbal behavior requires the development of a method of quantification so that "the psychological dimensions to be measured be precisely defined, that the historical cues be carefully pinpointed by which a receiver of any verbal messages infers the occurrence of any of these psychological states, and that the linguistic, principally syntactic, cues conveying intensity . . . be specified".

Gottschalk and his associates have attempted to determine the relationship of speech patterns to personality variables along three main avenues of approach. They have studied (1) the effect of specific stimuli on a subject's patterns, (2) the relationship between language patterns and psychodynamic patterns in patients undergoing psychoanalytic treatment, and (3) the differences in form and content variables among groups of persons differing in psychiatric diagnoses or in personality adjustment. The last focus of study has brought Gottschalk into the area of trait analysis. His investigation of schizophrenic speech, for example, relies upon verbal measures having a slow rate of change. Gottschalk has used both semantic and syntactic variables in the construction of his categories, believing that the exclusion of either one or the other would diminish greatly the sources of relevant data.

Chapter 2
Syntactic Correlates of Defense

In this chapter, we shall describe a method of identifying and measuring manifestations of psychological defense mechanisms in speech. We assume that individuals speaking under stressful conditions will demonstrate in their verbal behavior characteristic patterns of adaptation. In other words, habitual modes of coping are reflected in corresponding styles of speaking. To a great extent, what we call "personality" or "character" consists of observable ways of dealing with internal and external psychological stress. Traits like "courage," "cowardice," "apathy," and the like describe an individual's usual ways of resolving conflict and coping with danger. In a sense, psychiatric diagnosis is the grouping of patients according to defined styles of maladaptation to the vicissitudes of life. If our method can identify important adaptive mechanisms in speech successfully, we will have developed a useful tool for the study of personality.

Defense and Adaptation

Certain psychoanalysts distinguish the functions of defense and adaptation, attributing internal drive restriction to the former and the task of coping with the environment to the latter. We shall follow the suggestion of Anna Freud (1965) and use the two terms synonymously. Some of the adaptive responses we shall consider have been described as defense mechanisms in the psychoanalytic literature; others have not been so defined. All, however, are recognized widely by clinicians to be important and common ways of dealing with psychological stress.

Psychological defenses are not in themselves normal or pathological. A particular mechanism should be considered abnormal only if it is inappropriate to the age of the subject; is used to an inordinate degree, leading to a lack of adaptive balance; is too intense, resulting in excessive drive restraint; and is irreversible, that is, used to ward off old dangers that no longer exist (Freud, 1965, pp. 177–178). We believe that poor adaptive response to stress is reflected in the inappropriate or excessive use of certain speech mannerisms.

Grammatical Structures and Adaptation

As we have indicated already in Chapter 1, speech can be studied from a variety of viewpoints. The language component can be divided conveniently into the disciplines of (1) phonology, which describes how to put sounds together to form words; (2) syntax, which describes how sentences are formed from words; (3) semantics, which deals with the interpretations of the meaning of words and sentences; and (4) pragmatics, which describes how we participate in conversations. In addition to the verbal aspects of speech, there are the various nonverbal or paralinguistic phenomena. We refer to such variables as rate, pauses, amplitude, and pitch.

Of the variety of speech data available for analysis, syntactic and certain paralinguistic variables are most suitable for the study of stable personality characteristics. Semantic variables, on the other hand, have only limited usefulness for the identification of habitual adaptive responses. Although speakers do differ in their choice of vocabulary, such preferences are greatly influenced by a number of situational variables, notably topic of conversation (Laffal, 1965, p. 93). Other investigators have stressed the slow rate of change of a number of syntactic measures and their suitability for the study of characteristic behavior. Steingart & Freedman (1972), for example, have written:

> Common sense argues that what a person says is much more influenced by transient situational characteristics than how he says it. Therefore, as between language content and grammar, grammar would appear a priori to possess certain advantages for the exploration of . . . personality constructs. [p. 135]

While the study of meaning is not a useful way of identifying stable personality traits or habitual behavior, we believe that it is a suitable strategy for the investigation of psychological conflict and for the monitoring of psychotherapeutic processes.

Systems of verbal behavior analysis that depend upon the measurement of meaning often demand the exercise of subtle judgment on the part of scorers. Syntactic structures, being independent of meaning, lend themselves to easy recognition and measurement (Chomsky, 1957, p. 17). Compared to vocabulary preferences, a speaker's choice of grammatical forms is subject to less conscious manipulation, an important consideration when studying unconscious mechanisms of defense.

The degree to which practicing analysts rely upon paralinguistic and syntactic cues in their assessment of patients' defenses generally is not appreciated outside the psychoanalytic community. We believe that this is because most psychoanalytic writers tend to stress motivational factors contained in fantasies and dreams to the virtual exclusion of formal characteristics of speech. There have been some notable exceptions. Edelson, for example, recently has urged psychoanalysts to pay close attention to syntax in their interpretive work (1975).

Maria Lorenz, a clinician to whom we owe a great deal, drew the attention of her psychotherapist colleagues to the importance of grammatical structures in psychiatric diagnosis. Addressing herself to characteristic patient resistances in therapy, she pointed out that people who have psychological mechanisms in common also share habits of language use (Lorenz, 1955).

We assume that in a general way styles of speaking also reflect characteristic nonverbal behavior. We shall show in Chapter 4, for example, that impulsive individuals differ from more cautious people in the way they combine their words to form sentences. The correspondence between verbal and nonverbal behavior is, in all likelihood, not exact. We cannot ignore an individual's natural felicity for speaking. The act of speaking is extremely stressful for certain experimental subjects, and this may influence their choice of syntax in ways not yet obvious to us. We do not know whether speakers with severe speech pathology, such as stuttering and stammering, choose grammatical forms partly on the basis of their disabilities. Such individuals have been excluded from the various studies we have conducted.

Identifying Patterns of Adaptation in Free Speech

How can we recognize and measure clinically significant styles of adaptation in samples of free speech? We begin by assuming that well-defined patterns of behavior must be reflected somehow in significant deviations from the average frequency of certain paralinguistic and syntactic variables. Impulsive individuals, who make rapid, poorly planned decisions only to reverse them immediately afterwards, would be expected to use substantial numbers of adversative conjuctions, such as "but," "however," "although," and "nevertheless." Compulsive persons, who have to explain irrational acts, should make extensive use of causative conjunctions and phrases such as "because," "therefore," "in order to," and so on.

We do not assume that every use of an adversative or causative expression reflects impulsivity or rationalization respectively, only that individuals with impulsive and compulsive tendencies will choose such structures more frequently than persons not so disposed. Adversative and causative conjuctions and phrases are examples of grammatical structures that are recognized easily. Naive judges can be taught to identify and score them with relatively little training.

Collecting Samples of Free Speech:
Some Procedural Issues

What criteria should determine a method of data collection suited to the study of verbal expressions of defense? We prefer a standardized procedure to the sampling of naturally occurring speech in social conversations or psychotherapy because we intend to make intra-individual and intergroup comparisons. The mobilization of psychological defense mechanisms we seek requires an experimental task of more than routine difficulty and yet not so stressful that large numbers of subjects cannot master it. In this regard, we must pay particular attention to the special vulnerabilities of children and psychologically deviant adults. Since certain verbal characteristics of clinical interest appear relatively infrequently in spontaneous speech, we must carry out a statistical analysis over a sufficiently large sample of behavior (O'Dell & Winder, 1975). To avoid biasing the data in a certain direction, we prefer a nondirective method to one containing instructions subject to various interpretations by individuals of different ages and backgrounds. Finally, we believe that a procedure designed to elicit free, spontaneous speech is most suitable for the study of verbal mechanisms first noted in the course of psychotherapy. Uninterrupted monologue will provide us with the greatest variety of syntactic structures from which we can create our verbal categories.

We have found that a sample of approximately 1000 words is necessary to study the various form-dependent verbal mannerisms of interest to clinicians. At the ordinary rate of adult speech, this means an experimental period of 10 minutes. We have used the following standard procedure in all the clinical and developmental studies we have conducted to date.

After introducing himself, the experimenter explains to the subject that she will be asked to talk for 10 minutes on any topic or topics she chooses. The volunteer then is informed that neither will she be interrupted during the 10-minute period nor will the experimenter respond to questions until the procedure has been terminated. Following these introductory remarks, the subject is given a signal to begin speaking into a microphone that is attached visibly to a tape recorder. Her remarks are recorded for 10 minutes, during which time the experimenter refrains from both verbal communication and nonverbal signs of interest, encouragement, or disapproval. During the procedure, the experimenter and subject are alone in the speech laboratory. After the 10-minute sample has been recorded, it is transcribed, corrected, and analyzed.

We expected our data collection procedure to be difficult for many subjects but were surprised at how stressful most normal speakers found the task of talking uninterruptedly for 10 minutes. A number of volunteers, including U.S. military personnel with combat experience, described the experiment as one of the most frustrating tasks they had ever performed. The following verbatim remarks, taken from the monologues of 2 normal subjects, indicate how uncomfortable speaking spontaneously for 10 minutes can be.

Male subject: I'm at a standstill. (long pause) Are you going to stop it? (long pause) I can't think any longer. (long pause) Well, this recording, this testing just has caught me by surprise. I wasn't sure of what I was supposed to say or what I was supposed to do. And I'm at a blank at the moment. So this is all I can think of to say. I'm not much a man on talking. I never had nothing to talk about. That's my greatest problem. . . . Nothing comes to me on what to say.

Female subject: Turn it off! Can't you turn it off? Oh, please, my mind is a total blank. Can you—you turn it off and begin—let me begin again? . . . I can't think of anything else to say. Should I start on another subject? I'm certainly sorry that I hadn't prepared for this experiment. I—not very good at speaking freely on—without a given subject.

Despite the stress of the experimental procedure, nearly all subjects in the various groups we tested were sufficiently talkative to be included in the study. There were two exceptions. Approximately half of a group of normal children, aged five to seven, and half of a group of depressed psychiatric inpatients did not reach the required level of productivity.[1]

The Role of a Nondirective Experimenter

The principal reason we have the experimenter and subject in a room together is to provide a necessary stimulus for many volunteers, particularly children and ego-damaged adults. McGuire & Lorch (1968) have suggested that the "need to reduce tension between two people may be the driving force in initiating conversation." We believe that a second advantage in having the experimenter in the room is that it gives the subject an opportunity for verbal confrontation, a maneuver measured by one of our categories.[2]

Certain investigators have criticized the verbal analysis of monologues as an imcomplete and one-sided view of a communication process that involves two or more persons. According to these researchers, our method excludes one of the participants, the experimenter. We agree that communication between experimenter and subject occurs despite the absence of dialogue. Such a dyad, according to Jaffe, can be considered to be "a modified dialogue in which the flow of information is predominantly one-way. . . . The artificial separation . . . is valuable for experimental purposes, expecially if the goal is to define relatively stable personality traits. . . . This is best accomplished by holding certain interview parameters constant" (1961).[3]

The Control Group

The control group, with which we shall compare deviant populations in Chapter 4, was composed of 23 women employed or in training at the University of Maryland Hospital and 23 men serving in the U.S. armed forces. At the time we collected the speech samples, all subjects were between the ages of 18 and 45 and were drawn from a variety of occupations. Most were from a lower-middle-class background. The male volunteers were participating in a series of psychological studies and were interviewed by two psychiatrists to rule out serious psychopathology. Although we didn't fomally screen the female subjects, we had considerable information about their work and school performance; nobody known to be emotionally disturbed was included in the study. All control subjects had at least a high-school education and were free of gross speech pathology.[4]

Speech Categories

We created the following 14 categories from speech mannerisms that we believe reflect the operation of psychological coping mechanisms. These verbal maneuvers may indicate both reactions to psychological stress and attempts to master conflict-free cognitive tasks.

1. Quantity of speech.
2. Long pauses.
3. Rate of speech.
4. Nonpersonal references.
5. I.
6. We.
7. Me.
8. Negatives.
9. Qualifiers.
10. Retractors.
11. Direct references
12. Explainers.
13. Expressions of feeling.
14. Evaluators.

We claim no priority for the observation and description of the categorized speech mechanisms. All have been noted and reported in anecdotal ways by clinical investigators. What we have attempted is a more precise definition of the verbal reflections of psychological defensive operations so that naive judges can score them without extensive knowledge of lexical meaning. For readers interested in using our method, we have included a scored speech sample in Appendix A.[5]

Quantity of speech. We calculate productivity by counting all words spoken during the 10-minute experimental period. Only complete words are counted; incomplete words and sounds are ignored.

We believe that both extremes of verbal productivity can represent characteristic reactions to stress. Among psychopathological groups, volubility is common in manic, obsessional, and chronically anxious individuals. We have noted frequently the opposite tendency in certain depressed and impulsive persons.

In many instances, a speaker's productivity represents the pursuit of conscious goals. A fluent tongue can enhance greatly the effectiveness of entertainers, salesmen, and orators. Laconic responses are to be recommended to prisoners of war and poker players.

Long pauses. We classify as long pauses all intervals of more than five seconds during which no complete words are spoken. The final score for this category is obtained by adding the number of seconds in all pauses after having subtracted the first five seconds from each. If a subject, for example, pauses six times for periods of 2, 5, 4, 7, 6, and 18 seconds, the score is 16 seconds.

Frequent long pauses can be observed in a variety of psychiatric disorders, notably certain forms of depression and schizophrenia. In the course of psychotherapy, silence is often a reliable indicator of resistance and conflict, although the assertion that "silence seems best regarded as a defense" probably overstates the case (Mahl, 1956). Long pauses also may signal positive movement in psychotherapy; in otherwise talkative patients, silence is often an important part of the working-through process.

We should not ignore the many constructive uses of long pauses outside of therapy. Careful, precise conversationalists frequently pause to find the right word or phrase to express a thought. Silence serves an obvious self-protective function for those who distrust themselves. We tell lies as often in silence as with words. Silence can be used effectively to discourage the company of unwanted individuals and always has played an important role in female courtship behavior. A recent study of communication patterns among prostitutes and their clients demonstrates the conscious use of silence as a means of rejecting undesirable customers (Samovar & Sanders, 1978).

Several researchers have attributed to pauses a more general significance than mere resistance. Goldman-Eisler (1958) has demonstrated a positive association between pauses and the complexity of the material being discussed. Hesitations have been viewed as representing syntactic or encoding decisions (Boomer, 1970). Very long pauses, greater than 10 seconds, may serve different psychological functions than pauses of a few seconds (Siegman, 1978); the longer the silence, the greater the likelihood that it reflects resistance rather than simply information processing.[6]

Rate of speech. A measure of how quickly a subject speaks— while speaking—is obtained by dividing the total number of words uttered during the 10-minute period by the number of nonsilent minutes, calculated to the nearest 15 seconds. The number of nonsilent minutes is equal to 10, minus the final score for long pauses.

We may lose certain clinical distinctions if we do not eliminate long pauses when calculating rate of speech. Many depressed patients speak very slowly; certain schizophrenic and impulsive individuals speak at normal rates but with many long pauses; obsessional persons characteristically speak deliberately but without pausing at all. These nuances can be overlooked easily if we calculate rate by simply dividing the number of words by 10.[7]

There are sound clinical reasons for including rate of speech as a separate category. As we have suggested already, rate has been linked in the psychiatric literature to specific syndromes, notably several of the affective disorders. As both a state-dependent reaction in stress interviews and as a trait-dependent variable associated with the performance of chronically anxious individuals, accelerated speech has been identified as a sign of moderate anxiety. Studies have failed to demonstrate, on the other hand, increases in productivity or rate at very low or very high levels of anxiety (Murray, 1971).

Clinicians are familiar with the defensive uses of both rapid and slow speech. We wish to stress, however, the constructive uses of extreme speech rates in salesmanship, entertainment, news broadcasting, and oratory. Fluent individuals often use glibness as a conscious device to escape difficult situations. At times, a more deliberate style of speaking may be equally effective. We know of a former medical student who perfected the technique of answering difficult questions by droning on in a slow, measured cadence until his professors either fell asleep or lost interest.

We believe that individual differences in rate are due partly to unconscious, conflict-free factors concerned with information processing and articulation. We have every right to assume the same constitutional differences in retrieval, planning, and encoding that exist with respect to other cognitive processes dependent upon neuromuscular mechanisms.

Quantity of speech, long pauses, and rate of speech are properly designated as "paralinguistic" categories, since they are defined by neither semantic nor syntactic criteria. The remaining 11 measures depend primarily upon formal characteristics of verbal expression, and their scoring requires little or no familiarity with lexical meaning.

Nonpersonal references. We divide all clauses into "personal" and "nonpersonal." A "personal" clause is one whose subject refers to a person or persons conceivably known to and including the speaker. All other clauses are considered to be "nonpersonal," with the exception of those preceding indirect quotations, which are not scored in either category. Anatomical parts of individuals, reference to animals, and the use of universal subjects and impersonal pronouns all are scored as "nonpersonal."

The following examples illustrate the rules governing the scoring of statements in this category. (1) The statement is, "I think I'll go to the game." "I think" is not scored; "I'll go to the game" is scored as "personal." (2) The statement is, "Everybody likes ice cream." This clause is scored as "nonpersonal." (3) The statement is, "One has to drive carefully in heavy traffic." This clause is scored as "nonpersonal."

We obtain the final nonpersonal references score by dividing the number of nonpersonal references by the sum of nonpersonal and personal references and multiplying the quotient by 1000.

On the basis of clinical experience, we believe that both very high and very low nonpersonal references scores can reflect the operation of psychological defenses. An almost exclusive use of impersonal subjects in clause construction may well reflect the avoidance of intimacy and responsibility. In psychoanalytic therapy, according to Jaffe (1958), "the most extreme evidence of detachment is seen when the patient habitually communicates as a member of a group to the analyst as a member of another group." An example of this would be a patient saying to the therapist, "Analysts don't care about their patients," rather than "You don't care about me."

Infrequent use of nonpersonal references may reflect a certain concrete preoccupation with oneself and one's immediate family. In Chapter 4, we will present data demonstrating an inverse relationship between nonpersonal references and certain forms of psychopathology. A recently published study of seven patients in psychoanalysis, done by investigators using our verbal scales, showed an increased use of nonpersonal references over the course of therapy for all patients. This result may be due to a development of an observing ego as a consequence of psychoanalytic self-examination (Natale, Dahlberg, & Jaffe, 1978).

Is it possible that the use of nonpersonal references may be associated with educational achievement, particularly in scientific disciplines? Do individuals who have been trained to view their environment objectively and impersonally differ in their use of nonpersonal references from those who have not been educated similarly? We shall consider this question in Chapter 6, when we shall compare a group of medical students with subjects drawn from a variety of occupations.

I. We count all occurrences of the pronoun *I*, whether used alone or in contractions. Very high or low scores may indicate, respectively, self-preoccupation or detachment. Whereas "personal references" can include individuals other than the speaker, the use of *I* systematically excludes them. We believe that a moderate use of *I* reflects a healthy ability to commit oneself to thought and action while maintaining an adequate degree of self–object differentiation.

In general, clinical observers have agreed that infrequent use of *I* indicates avoidance of intimacy, commitment, and candor, whereas high frequency suggests inordinate self-preoccupation (Steingart & Freedman, 1972; Jaffe, 1960a).

We. All occurrences of this pronoun are scored, whether used alone or as part of a contraction. Unlike *I*, which almost always refers to the speaker, *we* can be used to designate the speaker and individuals known to the speaker (for example, "I met my wife and we went to the opera") or to refer to a poorly defined group of which the speaker is a member (for example, "World War II was long and bloody, but we finally won.") How a particular individual uses *we* can be ascertained from his nonpersonal references score. When both categories are high, the speaker probably is using *we* in a detached, impersonal way; a low nonpersonal references score accompanied by a high *we* score indicates a more intimate use of the pronoun.

We believe that a moderate *we* score suggests a healthy capacity to recognize and to collaborate with others. When the frequency of *we* is high and that of *I* is low, avoidance of commitment may be reflected, particularly if nonpersonal references are also common. A certain ratio of *I* to *we* may be a useful measure of mature self–object differentiation.

Me. We score all occurrences of the pronoun *me*. Little has been written about the use of this interesting pronoun. Spoken much less frequently than *I*, its significance for the psychology of speech is elusive and difficult to define. *Me* appears to be the most intimate of the personal pronouns. Unlike *I*, it is not used in automatic, impersonal ways by most speakers. If *I* represents the executive functions of the ego, *me* is closer to the concept of the self. Since *me* generally is used in passive grammatical constructions, it can reflect dependency and inactivity.

Negatives. We score without exception all negatives, such as "not," "no," "never," "nobody," and "nothing." Of our 14 categories, negatives have been associated most closely with a specific psychological mechanism in the psychoanalytic literature. Freud (1961) linked the use of negatives to the disavowal of forbidden wishes or memories. Although not every negative is a verbal expression of negation, we assume that speakers making frequent use of this mechanism will produce high negatives scores. The occurrence of negatives probably also is related to the defense mechanism of denial, which is not always clearly differentiated from negation by psychoanalytic writers. Denial generally refers to the disavowal of some aspect of external reality. By definition, negation always is framed in the negative, whereas denial also can be expressed affirmatively. An example of denial expressed affirmatively would be the coach of a losing football team exclaiming, "Our team is still the best!"

We wish to note the constructive use of negatives in the course of early childhood development and in normal adult functioning. The child's first "no" is an important milestone in the establishment of autonomous boundaries. The negative position continues throughout life to represent the ego's resistance to excessive intrusion, both from within and without. In a sense, we cannot say "yes" before we have learned to say "no." To give, we must first have something of our own. Anna Freud has noted that the idea of "mine" is associated with the child's achievement of individual status. Protection of his own possessions precedes the realization that others also have property (1965, p. 117).

Qualifiers. We score the following three kinds of speech mannerisms in this category: (1) expressions of uncertainty, for example, "*I think* that he is a pleasant companion"; (2) modifiers that weaken statements without adding information, for example, "That old house is *kind of* spooky"; and (3) phrases that contribute a sense of vagueness or looseness, for example, "Then we enjoyed *what you might call* an evening of riotous dissipation."

Qualifiers attributed to inidividuals other than the speaker are not scored, such as, "He thinks it will rain today." Verbs that are qualified in the past tense do not indicate uncertainty and are not counted, for example, "I thought you weren't coming."

We wish to point out that qualification is measured before the complete predicate is spoken. The message is, therefore, discounted before it is transmitted. When they occur in great frequency, qualifiers indicate a lack of decisiveness or an avoidance of commitment and responsibility (Nelson & Groman, 1975). Investigators generally assume that the use of qualifiers and other "ritualized" forms of speech increases with anxiety (Lalljee & Cook, 1975). Clinical researchers have stressed both the trait- and state-dependent aspects of qualification. In a clinical report, Jaffe (1960a) described two patients, one of whom was decisive, intolerant of ambiguity, and given to the use of few qualifiers in his speech. The other was characterized as "over-intellectualized and introspective . . . indecisive and action-inhibited"; his speech was "hesitant," full of "subjunctives and qualifiers."

The clinical observations of psychotherapists often are penetrating and insightful, but we must remember that their impressions
of patients' general behavior and mood may be influenced by the
very speech mannerisms they wish to study. This is true because
most therapists have direct access to patient behavior only during
psychotherapy sessions; under such constraints, it is almost impossible to make judgments about general behavior uninfluenced by
verbal style.

That qualifying is a useful and necessary aspect of normal
communication is apparent when we consider how dogmatic and
opinionated unqualified discourse sounds. Qualifiers facilitate the
expression of that which is tentative, hypothetical, and conditional.
Shadings, nuances, and subtleties of various kinds hardly could be
communicated without their use. Jaffe's "man of action," just referred to, supposedly lacked the "verbal and presumably the conceptual tools to make subtle discriminations." In a general way, tact and
diplomacy are greatly dependent upon the appropriate use of qualifiers. A very high frequency, however, may signal an inhibition of
decision, a paralysis of will.

Retractors. In this category, we score all expressions that par-
tially or totally retract immediately preceding statements, for example, "John is a real pest; of course, he's basically a nice person."
Expressions containing such adversative conjunctions as "but,"
"although," "however," and "nevertheless" almost invariably cancel
preceding remarks and are scored automatically. An example is,
"Your work has been unsatisfactory during the latter part of the
semester, *but* I shall give you a passing grade."

We believe that retractors reflect something close to the defense mechanism of "undoing." Their frequent use suggests difficulty in adhering to decisions already taken and imparts to the speaker's
verbal style a flavor of impulsivity. Unlike qualification, which
precedes and delays decision, retraction follows action already con-
summated.

Although the inordinate use of retractors suggests a style of
deviant behavior, moderate retraction in discourse reflects the
capacity for mature reconsideration, flexibility in judgment, and
openness to a broad range of possibilities. As in the case of qualification, speech without retraction has a certain barren and dogmatic

flavor. Investigators of language development in children consider expressions of qualification and retraction to be evidence of linguistic maturity, since they often occur in subordinate clauses (Loban, 1963). We shall consider the complex interaction of cognitive style and verbal defense more fully in Chapter 3.

Direct references. In this category we score all explicit references to (1) the experimenter, for example, "You're wearing a very nice suit"; (2) the experimental procedure, for example, "I never realized how long 10 minutes could be"; and (3) the physical surroundings, for example, "The paintings on the wall are beautiful." All questions directed at the experimenter, excluding obviously rhetorical ones, are scored, for example, "Is it all right to talk about my family?" An important rule is that consecutive direct references are not counted separately. If a subject, for example, discusses the tape recorder for 5 minutes without interruption, only one direct reference is counted; no more direct references are scored until an intervening statement is made on some subject other than the experiment, the experimenter, or the physical surroundings.

Gottschalk & Hambidge (1955) have compared the collection of spontaneous speech samples in the laboratory to a psychoanalytic session. To perform well, the subject must cope with his own considerable anxiety with little support from the experimenter, he must abide by the rules of the procedure, and he must derive whatever gratification he can from the experience without destroying his relationship with the silent companion in the room. According to these investigators, the subject's "verbal reactions are a partial expression of his total psychologic status at the moment. The verbal reactions are determined by a complex of factors. These factors include the past life experiences and reaction patterns that are mobilized in the process of adaptation to the situation".

We think that direct references reflect several maneuvers. Speakers with high scores in this category usually are indicating that they are having trouble carrying out the experimental procedure. Psychotherapists are familiar with patients' defensive preoccupation with the physical environment or the person of the therapist when trying to avoid introspective investigation. Certain subjects avoid embarrassing disclosures when taking word-association tests by naming objects in the room in response to verbal stimuli. Manipulative or despondent patients frequently make direct appeals for help, often exerting considerable pressure on the experimenter to abandon her defined role.

We regard the frequent occurrence of direct references as a reliable indication of a poorly functioning or immature ego. Normal subjects make direct references infrequently and almost always contain their anxiety sufficiently to "play the game" according to mutually agreed-upon rules.

We do not consider the complete absence of direct references in the course of a 10-minute monologue to be a reflection of mature adult performance. Occasional direct references may indicate a healthy curiosity and a capacity to confront the experimenter. In an interesting study, Jaffe (1960b) compared the personality characteristics of psychiatric inpatients, who mentioned the presence of a tape recorder during an initial interview, with those of a group of inpatients who did not. Compared to the "no-mention" group, those who referred to the tape recorder were described as younger, better-educated, more expressive, and less authoritarian. They also were considered to be more suitable psychotherapy candidates, whereas the "no-mention" patients were likely to be referred for somatic treatment.

Explainers. We score as an explainer any expression that (1) provides a reason or justification for an action, thought, or attitude or (2) indicates a causal connection of any kind. Causative conjunctions and phrases almost always are used as explainers, for example, "because," "as," "since," "in order to." They are scored automatically. This statement would be counted as an explainer: "I offered John the position *because* of his excellent work habits." Participial phrases frequently are used in explanatory ways, for example, "*Having lived in France for 20 years*, I can speak with authority on the subject of French cuisine."

We believe that *explainers* frequently are used for purposes of rationalization. Compared with operations like denial, projection, and undoing, which can be inferred frequently from nonverbal behavior, rationalization can be detected only from language behavior. Certain clinicians with a strong interest in verbal behavior have, in fact, assumed that explanatory expressions betray a predilection for rationalization. In a clinical report, Lorenz (1953) described a woman patient who made frequent use of connectives like "so," "therefore," "because," and "since." The author assumed that rationalization was one of the patient's main defense mechanisms.

Not all explaining is rationalization. Seeking security by proposing explanations for poorly understood phenomena is the most human of attributes and a necessary stiumulus to scientific reasoning. We can interpret the act of rationalization as an attempt to provide acceptable justification for thought and behavior the meaning of which has been obscured by repression and denial. Carried to extremes, rationalization almost always represents alienation from desire and signals a significant distortion of reality. We assume that excessive rationalizing tendencies are revealed by frequent occurrences of explainers in verbal behavior. Speech that is almost lacking in explainers, on the other hand, may appear concrete, dogmatic, and insensitive.

Expressions of feeling. In this category, we score all expressions in which the speaker describes himself as experiencing or having experienced some feeling. The range of scorable feelings is broad and includes the following: attraction–aversion; like–dislike; satisfaction–dissatisfaction; pleasure–displeasure; hope–despair. Other expressions of feeling that we count are fear, anger, desire, and so on. The following are examples of scorable expressions of feeling: (1) "*I love* classical music"; (2) "Your birthday card *pleased me* very much"; and (3) "*I was disgusted* by his boorish behavior."

We do not score impersonal references to feelings, such as, "It was a terrifying incident." Expressions of interest, physical sensations, and conditional feelings are not scored, for example, "I would be delighted to attend if invited."

Experienced clinicians are sensitive to degrees of affective display when assessing characteristic reactions to stress. Certain patients avoid unpleasant detail by flooding their therapists with histrionic emotion; others speak only in a carefully reasoned, "logical" manner, no matter how anxious and depressed they may otherwise appear.

We hardly need to stress the importance of expressions of

feeling in normal discourse. How vital they are for the building and maintaining of empathic relationships becomes clear when we meet people who use few feeling words. How cold, distant, and mechanical they seem! Those who use feeling words to an extreme, however, often impress their listeners as insincere and superficial.

Evaluators. We score all expressions of judgment in the following areas: (1) goodness–badness, for example, "He's the *best* worker in the organization"; (2) usefulness–uselessness, as in, "Your idea *won't work*"; (3) right–wrong, for example, "It is *sinful* to steal"; (4) correct–incorrect, as in, "You have the *right* answer"; (5) propriety–impropriety, as in, "You *should not* dress that way for a wedding"; (6) pleasant–unpleasant, for example, "It's *nice* to be on vacation in June"; and (7) exclamatory phrases expressing opinions, such as, "What a *great* town!"

Expressions of judgment in the following areas are not scored: (1) easy–difficult, (2) industrious–lazy, and (3) interesting–dull. Evaluators are not scored when used as quantifiers, as in, "That's a good-sized bed."

Although our exclusion of certain kinds of evaluators may appear arbitrary, we believe that such a practice eliminates many conflict-free judgments. In this way, the category probably more narrowly reflects superego and ego-ideal functions.

Evaluators do not reflect any specific, well-known defense mechanisms. We know, however, that individuals differ in their use of these expressions and such variations have diagnostic implications. Since evaluators include a number of different but related areas of judgment, we must interpret their use very cautiously. In our opinion, high scores in this category reflect the existence of a severe, tyrannical conscience, a point of view that is shared by other students of verbal behavior. Lorenz (1953) has written of the verbal style of a phobic patient: "The 'should' note was struck again and again during interviews. Rigid superego demands and restrictions were involved in his neurotic conflicts."

We believe that greater precision will be achieved if this category is subdivided further in order to separate moral judgments from expressions of convenience. More will be said about this problem in Chapter 8.

Determination of Final Scores

The final scores for the last 10 categories are calculated by converting raw scores into numbers of scored units per 1000 words and rounding off to one decimal point. (Example: Subject speaks 400 words and has a raw score of 3; the corrected score is 7.5.)[8]

Interjudge Scoring Agreement

For all categories in which scoring is not automatic, agreement has ranged from 70 percent for retractors to 94 percent for negatives (Weintraub & Aronson, 1962). We should note that the percentages were obtained by dividing the number of items scored by both judges for each category by the number of items scored by either judge. This results in a conservative estimate of agreement, since items that both judges considered unscorable were not credited.

Intrasubject Reliability

We subjected all 14 categories to a test of intra-individual reliability by collecting a second 10-minute speech sample from each of 14 male controls one week after the initial data were gathered. Intra-individual reliability was reached for all 14 categories at a level of significance of at least $p < .05$ (Weintraub & Aronson, 1962).[9]

Interscale Correlational Analysis

Although no attempt was made to correlate the performance of the controls in all 14 categories, we did a number of interscale comparisons where significant findings were anticipated.

We found that quantity of speech varied inversely with long pauses ($r = -0.84$, $df = 21$, $p < .01$) and showed a positive association with rate of speech ($r = 0.89$, $df = 21$, $p < .01$). Long pauses and rate of speech showed a significant negative correlation. These findings indicated that the more rapid the speech and the fewer the long pauses, the greater was the total productivity. Those individuals whose speech was punctuated by long pauses also had frequent hesitations of under 5 seconds.

Direct references showed significant negative correlations with quantity of speech ($r = -0.67$, $df = 21$, $p < .01$) and rate of speech ($r = -0.49$, $df = 21$, $p < .05$) and a positive association with long pauses ($r = 0.79$, $df = 21$, $p < .05$). These findings confirmed our speculation that a high direct references score reflects a subject's difficulty in carrying out the experimental procedure. According to Spence (1973), patients in psychoanalysis show an inverse relationship between productivity and explicit references to the analyst. When a theme is closest to awareness, "the analytic process is operating poorly, presumably because the patient is not able to control the emerging anxiety." When the content is well disguised, according to Spence, "it does not disrupt the stream of associations."

We found a positive association between quantity of speech and both negatives ($r = 0.65$, $df = 17$, $p < .01$) and retractors ($r = 0.50$, $df = 21$, $p < .05$). The last two categories were correlated strongly with each other ($r = 0.63$, $df = 17$, $p < .01$). We believe this indicates that glib speech may be partly defensive; some of what is said is being negated, denied, and retracted. Nelson & Groman (1975) have reported that subjects may avoid silence by means of voluble, defensive speech.

Qualifiers and retractors showed a positive correlation ($r = 0.43$, $df = 21$, $p < .05$), a result that did not surprise us in view of the similar defensive functions they serve. One neutralizes the force of an act before it is taken; the other seeks to undo an already-executed act.

Expressions of feeling showed a positive association with the pronoun *I* ($r = 0.57$, $df = 21$, $p < .01$) and an inverse relationship with nonpersonal references ($r = -0.57$, $df = 21$, $p < .01$). This result was partly a consequence of our scoring system, which requires that feelings be attributed directly to the speaker, and partly a reflection of the detachment accompanying impersonal content.

Another finding we wish to note is the lack of positive association between the personal pronouns *I* and *me*. Some of the possible psychological differences between the two already have been discussed. They apparently serve different defensive purposes, the nature of which will become clearer when we compare the speech patterns of males and females and analyze the verbal behavior of deviant populations.

Summary

We have demonstrated that it is possible to define and measure a number of speech characteristics that apparently are related to psychological defense mechanisms. The categories described have been created primarily from clinical anecdotes reported in the literature and from personal observations gathered in the course of psychoanalytic practice. Both syntactic and paralinguistic aspects of speech can be scored by independent judges, with acceptable levels of agreement. A group of normal, male volunteers tested twice at weekly intervals achieved significant intra-individual reliability in all categories. Interscale correlations revealed a number of significant relationships among the various categories, some predictable, some unexpected. At the very least, we can state that inferences about personality and behavior can be drawn from an intensive analysis of the formal characteristics of free speech.

We have not been able to control strictly for all variables that conceivably may affect patterns of verbal behavior. Subjects were not matched for intelligence or socioeconomic background, although all volunteers had at least a high-school education. By limiting the categories to simple syntactic structures in general use by preschool children, we assume that intellectual and class differences do not affect significantly their frequency of occurrence. In subsequent chapters, we shall present additional data to support this assumption.

Psychotherapists and diagnosticians intuitively take verbal style into account in their daily work with patients. They know that individuals diagnosed as "depressed," "schizophrenic," and "compulsive" speak differently, although these differences are not always easy to define. In Chapter 4, we shall examine systematically the verbal behavior of psychologically deviant groups. First, however, the variables of age and sex will be considered.

Notes

1. On the whole, the performance of both normal and deviant subjects has justified our strategy of stimulating verbal productivity by the use of a nondirective, anxiety-provoking procedure. Data published by other investigators have generally shown a positive association between speech productivity, on the one hand, and anxiety and nondirective procedures on the other (Benton, Hartman, & Sarason, 1955; Kanfer, 1959; Pope & Siegman, 1965). Although a nondirective approach is undoubtedly more stressful for certain individuals than for others, it has the advantage of provoking an adequate level of anxiety against which are mobilized a broad array of psychological defenses.

2. Placing the experimenter in the same room as the subject may introduce an uncontrollable source of bias. Reports published by students of nonverbal behavior suggest that patterns of communication of one member of a dyad may be influenced by the sex, status, gaze, gestures, and proximity of the other member (Buck et al., 1972; Kendon, 1970; Scheflen, 1965; Sommer, 1967). Although there is little evidence that formal characteristics of speech are modified by such variables, the possibility cannot be excluded (Williams, 1970).

   In order to control for the possible effects of visual communication between experimenter and subject, we collected 10-minute speech samples from 12 normal male subjects on two occasions. For each subject, one sample was collected with the experimenter sitting opposite him and the other with the experimenter placed behind him, hidden from view. The two samples were collected at one-week intervals with the variable of the experimenter's position controlled for the effect of order. In none of the verbal categories did we find significant differences between the two sets of data.

3. Dyadic communication does not require the conscious two-way transmission of messages but may be seen "as an interaction in which both participants are inescapably members in a system governed by rules" (McGuire & Lorch, 1968). We have facilitated the standardization of our data-gathering procedure by keeping the activity of one of the participants, the experimenter, as constant as possible in order to study the speech pattern of the subject.

4. The male controls included officers and enlisted men ranging in rank from private to major; both career soldiers and draftees were included in the group. Their military assignments varied in sophistication from simple clerical tasks to complex intelligence work. The female control subjects were drawn from the ranks of medical students, nurses, activity therapists, secretaries, and clerks. Both male and female controls were, therefore, heterogeneous for occupation and level of education. They came from all regions of the country and included individuals of urban, suburban, and rural origins. All except one male subject were born in the United States and spoke English as their native tongue. We made no attempt to match the male and female subjects for specific demographic characteristics.

5. All categories meet the following five criteria. (1) In order to measure stable

personality characteristics, we created categories based upon syntactic and para-linguistic variables having a slow rate of change. (2) Scoring is generally objective and in a number of categories is automatic, thus ensuring adequate interjudge agreement. (3) All categories have been linked explicitly or implicitly in the literature to psychological defense or coping mechanisms. (4) All speech manner-isms occur frequently enough in a 10-minute monologue to permit statistical analysis of groups of transcripts. Bizarre, rare speech phenomena, which may be almost pathognomonic for certain disorders, have not been included. Since the preliminary work necessary for the construction of the categories was done with nondeviant volunteers, all verbal mannerisms are in general use by normal speak-ers. (5) In order to minimize the effects of subjects' intelligence and education on performance, complex grammatical forms requiring extensive subordination have not been used in category construction.

6. Our procedure calls for the measurement of long pauses by the manual operation of a stopwatch. Although this method may appear crude to readers familiar with automated electronic measurements of silent pauses, correlations of 0.80 and better have been reported between manual and electronic techniques. This suggests that, for long hesitations, elaborate and expensive devices may be unnecessary (Sieg-man, 1978). In any case, a category that ignores nonverbal vocalizations like grunts, coughs, and incomplete words cannot be adapted easily to automated, electronic monitoring.

7. Other investigators have addressed themselves to this problem by distinguishing a "speech rate," obtained by dividing the number of words by the time available to speak, from an "articulation rate," calculated by dividing the number of words by phonation time (Natale, 1977).

8. Since preliminary studies found that intra-individual reliability is not achieved under conditions of relatively low word frequency, *negatives* and *explainers* are scored only for those subjects speaking 600 and 800 words respectively. Intra-individual reliability for all other verbal categories was achieved at the level of 200 words.

9. We included the personal-pronoun categories in our system after the publication of the original data. The reliability data for the three pronouns are: I ($r = 0.63$, $df = 12$, $p < .05$); We ($r = 0.86$, $df = 12$, $p < .01$); and Me ($r = 0.64$, $df = 12$, $p < .05$).

Chapter 3
Developmental Aspects of Speech and Personality

Walter Weintraub, M.D. and
S. Michael Plaut, Ph.D.

If the speech categories we described in Chapter 2 reflect styles of adaptation, they should mirror the rapid and dramatic personality changes that occur in childhood and adolescence. Since we have created most of our categories from grammatical structures used by small children, their frequency of occurrence at different ages should be sensitive to the periodic shifts in equilibria among drives and defenses, as well as to the more orderly and progressive maturing of conflict-free cognitive processes. To the extent that emotional factors influence the use of speech mechanisms, we must be prepared to observe at certain critical age periods evidence of verbal regression and disorganization, as well as of maturation and integration.

A comparison of the speech habits and general behavior of children and adolescents will enable us to test some of the assumptions we made in Chapter 2 relative to the association of verbal behavior and mechanisms of adaptation. In some instances, our data may challenge certain generally accepted developmental notions, many of which are based upon clinical observations.

The research strategy we have adopted is similar to the one we used in Chapter 2. We shall compare samples of free speech collected from groups of children and adolescents at critical age periods, when changes in the relative strengths of drive and defense can be expected to be reflected in corresponding alterations in verbal style. In order to avoid as much as possible the effects of situational variables, we have included in our study only groups of children mature enough to provide speech samples under the experimental conditions we described in the previous chapter. Before discussing the results of our developmental studies, we shall review briefly some basic concepts of language acquisition in infancy and early childhood.

The Development of Speech in Childhood

Preverbal Communication

Although linguists and developmental psychologists have investigated the manner in which children learn to speak, certain mechanisms of language acquisition are poorly understood. The beginnings of speech in infancy precede by many months the ability of the child to comprehend and use words as signs and symbols. We owe to Vygotsky (1962) the notion that speech has a long preintellectual stage during which the sounds uttered by the child are not yet associated with stable mental representations of corresponding objects.

Clinicians have observed forms of social communication that precede even the most primitive vocal exchanges. Within a few days after birth, we can see synchronized movements between many mothers and their babies. This early nonvocal exchange of messages may be the precursor of the phenomenon of interactional synchrony, in which the flow of movement in the listener is coordinated rhythmically with the verbal behavior of the speaker (Condon & Ogston, 1966; Kendon, 1970). We welcome these early synchronous movements as a possible indication of a "good fit" between mother and baby (Brazelton, 1974).

The infant's cooing and babbling, which we may think of as the beginnings of speech, do not appear, at first, to serve the purpose of communication. These early sounds have little to do with self-induced or social auditory stimuli and are identical among congenitally deaf and hearing children. Mothers, of course, generally do impute to their babies certain wishes and needs from these early sounds, a tendency that undoubtedly helps develop and strengthen affective bonds (Freedman, 1972).

At about the tenth week of age, infants begin to respond affectively to sounds. We can begin to note mutual gaze and vocalization exchanges as "evidence for the specialized early perception of speech sounds and for the establishment of mother–child communication patterns" (Nelson, 1977a). Within the first few months of life, infants can discriminate among speech stimuli and, prior to the beginning of language, can indicate their internal state and intentions by means of subtle cues (Mahl, 1964). During this early period, mother's spoken words probably are experienced as tones and rhythms, rather than as words with meanings (Lewis, 1977). A baby is extraordinarily skillful in differentiating nuances in its mother's mood. Anxious or angry behavior on the part of the mother may be associated with irritability and signs of insecurity in the infant (Milmoe et al., 1968).

As spontaneous, internally generated vocalizations are brought progressively under auditory control, we can begin to distinguish the babbling of the normal infant from the more restricted range of sounds of the congenitally deaf baby. These differences can be noted clearly as early as the sixth month (Lenneberg, 1964). The ability to develop normal speech sounds depends upon the establishment of vocal–auditory connections, which can be demonstrated as early as the fourth month. As the sounds of the baby are used increasingly as auditory stimuli, it succeeds in monitoring its own vocalizations and develops its innate potential for speech (Edelheit, 1969).

Early Mechanisms of Speech Acquisition

Although recognizable words usually are not spoken before the first birthday, infants do begin to act in a discriminating way toward certain words in the last quarter of the first year. At first, these words are "embedded in a context rich in extra-linguistic cues"; later the words are responded to as independent signals (Nelson, 1977a).

There is general agreement among investigators that all children follow the same sequence in the development of language skills. Comprehension precedes performance by approximately six months. As Chomsky (1964) has concluded, "There is no doubt that the child's achievements in systematizing linguistic data, at every stage, go well beyond what he actually produces in normal speech . . . advances are generally 'across the board.' " This is particularly true for the child's mastery of the phonological system of adult speech, which is far advanced before the end of the babbling period. During the second half of the first year, before the first word has been uttered, the infant already has learned the intonation contours of his native tongue (Moskowitz, 1978).

In addition to motor skills, speech requires a certain level of comprehension of both phonological and syntactical aspects of language. The mechanisms by which children begin and continue to talk remain a mystery. Hymes has hypothesized that the human brain has built into it a "language generator" that is "primed to go off when suitable samples of speech are presented to it" (1964).

Assimilation of Adult Grammatical Structures

To learn to speak a language, a child must communicate actively with real people who are fluent in that language. It apparently is impossible for him to learn solely from television, for example, because codable discrepancies between the child's current syntactic structures and those used by individuals more familiar with the language will go unnoticed. Incorporation of new forms into an immature linguistic system requires live conversationalists who can respond to the child's answers (Nelson, 1977b).

According to the nativist theory of language acquisition, proposed by Chomsky (1964) and Lenneberg (1964), the structures and functions of the nervous system essential to the learning of language are present at birth. The opportunity for interaction with speaking individuals is the only necessary environmental contribution (Menyuk, 1969).

In the course of acquiring an adult grammar, children pass through a number of stages in which they make systematic "errors."

These "errors" are not incorrect imitations of adult speech but are correct and grammatical with respect to the child's current grammar. Children do not immediately learn "correct" adult grammar because of conceptual limitations. Because they will not use grammatical forms they do not understand, children must pass through stages of syntactic development associated with an increasing ability to abstract grammatical rules from samples of speech. A child cannot use the future tense before the past tense, for example, because the notion of "future" is vastly more difficult from a conceptual point of view than the idea of "past." This explains why, as Moskowitz (1978) puts it, "children are fairly impervious to the correction of their language by adults" and why it is so difficult to teach children a detail of language before they are ready to learn it themselves. The extent to which language development can be influenced by environmental factors is a controversial issue that has been stimulated recently by published data supporting a heritability factor in syntactical development (Munsinger & Douglass, 1976), a claim that has been challenged vigorously (Fahey, Kamitomo, & Cornell, 1978; Munsinger, 1978).

Behaviorists have tried to explain the mechanisms of language acquisition on the basis of imitation and reinforcement. Behaviorist explanations cannot account, however, for the appearance among young children of completely novel grammatical structures (Osser, 1970).

Speech development proceeds predictably through stages of one-word, two-word, three-word, and short telegraphic sentences in which grammatical relations are expressed through fixed word order rather than by the use of function words. Small children exercise a certain control over the speech of adults by noncomprehension feedback. This limits the occurrence of a structure in remarks addressed to them by adults. The child then "imitates and reduces that structure," which is subject to affirmation or correction by the more linguistically mature listener. As the child's comprehension of a particular structure increases, his feedback allows a higher rate of occurrence in adult speech. At about the same time, the new structure begins to appear in his own spontaneous speech (Bohannon & Marquis, 1977).

Level of Syntactic Development
of the Preschool Child

All of the basic grammatical forms we used to create the verbal categories outlined in Chapter 2 occur in the spontaneous speech of five-year-old children. Most investigators agree that, at the age of five,

> the child will have achieved control of a remarkably high proportion of the adults' system for sentence production and comprehension. The same words, the same dimensions, and the same kinds of sentence structures that adults use, generally can be used by the five-year-old. Moreover, the child at five is capable of using this system with high success even when other contextual support is minimal. In using the system to communicate, the five-year-old, like the adult, retains the meanings of prior sentences in a conversation, while generally forgetting the sentence structure which carried the meanings. [Nelson, 1977b]

We must not assume that the use of "adult" constructions by five-year-olds reflects mature comprehension of syntactic relations. Kindergarten and first-grade children, for example, lack complete understanding of some of the connectives they use in their spontaneous speech. Temporal relations of "because" are better understood than causal ones. Adversative connectives like "but" and "although" also are incompletely comprehended (Hutson & Shub, 1975; Palermo & Molfese, 1972).

Language Development in
Adolescence and Adulthood

Linguists and psychologists have given far more attention to the development of language and speech among preschool children than to the verbal behavior of latency-aged children and adolescents. We know almost nothing about syntactic changes occurring with increasing age in the postadolescent years. Certain investigators have suggested that significant grammatical changes cease to occur after late adolescence (Hunt, 1970), but we believe such a conclusion to be premature in view of the paucity of published data. We might at the very least expect some modifications in the language of elderly subjects, even among those not suffering from organic brain disease, because of the neurophysiological effects of normal aging.

Although researchers have published few studies of spontaneous speech among children of school age, available data indicate that important syntactical changes continue to occur with increasing age, at least until late adolescence. These changes consist primarily in the production of longer clauses and the greater use of subordination (Hunt, 1970; Loban, 1963).

Sex Differences in Language Performance

Certain investigators have reported female superiority in all aspects of language performance that show developmental trends with age. These differences in favor of girls can be identified as soon as children begin to speak (McCarthy, 1930, 1953). It is well known that language difficulties, such as dyslexia and stuttering, are far more frequent among boys. Other researchers have denied sexual differences in language acquisition, particularly with respect to the use of basic syntactic structures. Menyuk (1969), for example, has attributed reports of female language superiority to poorly controlled experimenter and situational variables.

Some Procedural Issues in the Study of Children's Speech

We had to resolve two major procedural issues before applying our method to children's speech. First of all, we decided not to include groups of preschool children in our study. The inclusion of children under the age of five would have required modifications of our experimental procedure, which is not supportive enough for preschoolers. Numerous language studies already have been carried out among the very young, whereas the literature contains very few reports of systematically gathered spontaneous speech from school-aged children and adolescents. We believe that greater clarification of language performance will be forthcoming if we use a standard technique that "moves backward from adult speech through older children toward younger ones. It may be that the few differences that are found will turn out to be formulatable in relatively simple terms" (Lees, 1964). Another point we must consider is the fact that the frequency of occurrence of even simple grammatical structures is so dependent upon cognitive, maturational factors in preschool children that the influence of emotional variables may be extremely difficult to determine. If we limit our study of speech to children and adolescents of school age, changes in the use of verbal mechanisms developed from simple grammatical structures should reflect the interaction of intellectual and emotional variables, particularly as they undergo typical alterations at critical age periods.

The second procedural issue concerned the choice of critical age periods during which significant changes in language perform-ance, as reflections of rapid cognitive development and emotional upheaval, could be expected to occur. Students of language believe that transitional periods, characterized by loss or modification of old structures and by progress to higher levels of understanding and performance, are found between the ages of 5 and 7 and from 12 to 14 years (O'Connell, Griffen, & Norris, 1967; Palermo & Molfese, 1972). In addition to these 2 age periods, we chose 2 others as worthy of investigation: latency, from ages 9 to 11, and midadoles-cence, from ages 15 to 17.[1]

Gathering Free-Speech Samples from Children, Adolescents, and Adults

We collected 10-minute samples of spontaneous speech from groups of children in the following age periods: 5–7, 9–11, 12–14, and 15–17. Using the same method of data collection described in Chap-ter 2, we asked each subject to talk for 10 minutes on any subject or subjects she wished. Two experimenters, one male and one female, collected the samples from the young subjects. For each age group, half the volunteers of both sexes were tested by the male technician, half by the female experimenter.

We selected the volunteers for the study from a private, coedu-cational school in the Baltimore area. The school is college prepara-tory and enrolls on one campus students from kindergarten through high school. Although the student body represents a wide range of intelligence and temperament, the majority are white, middle or upper class, and of Anglo-Saxon, Christian background. We can assume safely that no mentally retarded or severely disturbed children were included in the study.

To complete the "life cycle," we decided to add to the 4 child and adolescent groups 46 normal adults, aged 18–45, who have alredy been described in Chapter 2, and a group of senior citizens over the age of 60. Twenty volunteers, 10 females and 10 males, comprised each of the 4 school-aged and senior citizen groups. The 18–45 group included 23 men and 23 women.

Both adult groups were primarily from a lower-middle-class background, and were therefore somewhat below the private-school subjects in socioeconomic standing. The senior citizens ranged in age from 60–85. All were living in their own homes or apartments and were relatively free of grossly disabling physical and psychological illnesses.

Collecting Free-Speech Samples from Early Schoolers

Is it reasonable to expect a kindergarten or first-grade pupil to generate free speech for 10 minutes in the presence of a nontalking adult? Although children between the ages of 5 and 7 are beginning to use mature grammatical forms, they often lack the "internal distancing" necessary to speak about a need independently of the wish to have that need gratified (Lewis, 1977); yet, our procedure required of the experimenters that they gain the cooperation of the young volunteers without allowing themselves to be used as need-satisfying objects. We encountered the same problem when studying the speech patterns of ego-damaged adults, many of whom expect and demand support from the experimenter. Although our procedure proved to be too demanding for a number of early schoolers, enough of them were able to tolerate the stress of the experiment to allow comparisons with the other groups in almost all categories.

Age-Related Themes

Almost all subjects in the various age groups, with the exception of the youngest, were able to follow satisfactorily the data-collection procedure and to provide the required minimum of 200 words. Of the 20 children in the 5- to 7-year-old age group, only 11 spoke enough to be included in the study. In several instances, we were not able to transcribe tapes of subjects in certain of the older age groups because of technical difficulties. The exact number of volunteers in each group for whom we have usable data is shown in Table 3–1.

Before discussing the results of our study, we shall describe briefly the major topics discussed by the subjects in the various age groups. Such a description will provide us with a thematic context for the subsequent consideration of significant differences in the various verbal categories.

Early Schoolers

We recruited the children in this group from kindergarten and first grade. Seven of the 10 boys were able to speak 200 or more words; only 4 of 10 girls could meet the minimum productivity requirement. This confirmed the impression that young female children are somewhat more shy than males (McCarthy, 1930). We were surprised by the variety of behaviors demonstrated by the early schoolers, some acting in a rather poised, mature manner, others in more aggressive, playful ways. The girls all were polite and agreeable.

Table 3–1. Number of Speech Samples in Each Age Group Used in Statistical Analyses.

Group	Age	Males	Females
Early Schoolers	5–7	7	4
Latency Children	9–11	8	9
Young Adolescents	12–14	10	10
Midadolescents	15–17	8	8
Adults	18–45	23	23
Senior Citizens	60–85	10	10

When they failed to meet the requirements of the experiment, their inability or unwillingness to speak was not accompanied by other forms of regressive behavior. They simply remained silent and left the room when excused by the experimenter. Those who did speak described certain events of their daily lives. Other than themselves, the principal characters in their monologues included parents, siblings, relatives, and school and neighborhood friends. (Since the neighborhood is often at a considerable distance from the school, the private-school children commonly had two sets of friends.) Curiously, no pets were mentioned by any of the early schoolers, although almost all families with children in the private school had one or more animals in their homes. One of the girls spent part of her time recounting a long Bible story; another took about half of the 10 minutes to describe various objects in the experimental room. Several girls complained about the difficulty of finding a topic to discuss.

A few boys who spoke the minimum number of words also spent most of their time discussing school and neighborhood activities, parents, toys, vacations, and outings. Their monologues contained no references to pets. Two male subjects recited long stories, over and over again, until the 10-minute period was completed. One told the story of "The Three Little Pigs" repeatedly, using almost identical words each time; the other created an interesting account of his own life cycle from birth to death, including in the recitation the major events he expected to experience. This fantasy, which was about 200 words long, was repeated without modification 4 times during the 10-minute period.

Two boys spent the entire experimental session complaining about the procedure and insulting the experimenter. They were remarkably playful and uninhibited, as the following verbatim excerpts indicate:

> *First boy:* Shut up, you monkey. . . . Get out before I hit you. . . . This has been a recording of your silly recording. . . . So long, folks, this has been a recording of your silly quack quack.

> *Second boy:* Get out of here or I'll karate your rear end off. . . . Good-bye, dodo brain. See you, see you all later. So long, alligator, in a while crocodile. Bye-bye, rotten egg, dodo brain, dummy do-do. . . . What's up, Doc?

Only the early schoolers spoke in such unrestrained ways. The latency children and adolescents invariably were polite and respectful. Several of the latter, however, were quite playful in a much more articulate and sophisticated manner.

Latency Children

We recruited the 20 children in this group from the fourth and fifth grades. They ranged in age from 9 to 11, and, with the exception of 1 girl, all spoke the minimum number of 200 words. We could not use 2 of the boys' tapes, however, because of technical problems.

The approach of the latency children to the experimental task was dramatically different from that of the early schoolers. They were remarkably sober and businesslike. In contrast to the behavior of the early schoolers, there was not a single example of playfulness, overt hostility, complaining, or confrontation. The few references to the experimental procedure (there were none to the experimenter) consisted of comments or questions about the amount of time remaining in the session. With several exceptions to be noted later, the latency children developed themes similar to those of the early schoolers. They talked a good deal about school and neighborhood activities, family vacations, and so forth, although these topics were discussed in a less self-centered way. While the early schoolers could speak only of incidents in which they participated (with the exception of those with prepared stories like "The Three Little Pigs"), the latency children were able to discuss events that occurred in their absence.

The latency children, particularly the girls, often mentioned their pets. All 9 girls and 4 of the 8 boys spoke about animals, some in very great detail. There were other sex differences in the latency children's themes. The girls spoke more about their homes, teachers, and books. They discussed boys' school activities, whereas the boys rarely mentioned girls outside their families. Several of the girls showed a sensitive awareness of interpersonal problems, a concern that did not appear in the boys' monologues. The boys were more preoccupied with organized school and neighborhood sports and mechanical devices such as scooters, boats, and motorcycles.

Latency children of both sexes showed little evidence of introspection or psychological conflict. They appeared to be organized and functioning well in school and at home. Although some of the girls clearly were noticing boys, heterosexual social activities were not discussed. Members of both sexes were directing their energies toward school, family, and peers of the same sex. Latency children approached the experimental procedure in as matter-of-fact and routine a way as they appeared to be managing their daily activities. If some of the group found the task stressful, they nevertheless executed it without complaint or confrontation.

Our experience with the latency children coincides almost exactly with the profile of the 10-year-old published by the Yale Study Group: "In a frank, unself-conscious manner, he tends to accept life and the world as they are with free and easy give-and-take. It is a golden age of developmental equipoise" (Gesell, Ilg, & Ames, 1956, p. 37).

Early Adolescents

We recruited the subjects in this age group from the seventh and eighth grades. All 20 volunteers spoke the minimum 200 words, and transcripts for the entire group were available for analysis. Compared to the early schoolers and latency children, the early adolescents demonstrated a wider interest in and understanding of the world outside the immediate family. Although they mentioned parents, siblings, relatives, and pets, academic and athletic competition was probably the single most important theme recurring in their speech samples. Peer activities of various kinds during school sessions and vacation became more prominent, while teachers and other important adults outside the family also were mentioned frequently. Although the early adolescents showed interest in the opposite sex, comments about teen-aged romance were brief and infrequent.

Philosophical and political questions preoccupied several of the early adolescents. They freely discussed such topics as racial prejudice, the meaning of Christmas, and the state of the national economy. As a group, the early adolescents were much more introspective than the early schoolers and latency children. Several, for example, described psychological reactions to the stresses of scholastic and athletic competition; others spoke with sensitivity and insight of family conflicts. School dramatics was a significant topic for a number of early adolescents of both sexes. Food was an important subject for a few of the boys, an observation made by other investigators of young adolescents (Gesell, Ilg, & Ames, 1956).

A number of the early adolescents reverted to the playful activities of the early schoolers, although the hostility was well disguised. Both boys and girls in this group seemed more uncomfortable with the procedure than the latency children. Several appeared extremely uneasy and resorted to discussing objects in the room in order to pass the time. There was a good deal of self-conscious preoccupation with social impressions, as evidenced by the following excerpts:

> *Girl:* I'm making an idiot out of myself. . . . I'm wrecking the tape because I have nothing to say. . . . She's looking at me as if I'm some kind of idiot. . . . Oh God! I hope I don't have much more time left.

> *Boy:* I enjoy talking, but I like to have someone answering me so it doesn't look like I'm talking to myself, like I'm crazy.

The early adolescents showed a number of nonverbal signs of embarrassment and uneasiness, such as giggling, blushing, and fidgeting. Compared to the latency children, they had more trouble containing their anxiety. Although functioning well at home and at school, they showed definite signs of conflict within themselves and with the world around them.

Midadolescents

The 20 subjects in this group were all second- and third-year high-school students. They ranged in age from 15 to 17. Although all spoke the minimum 200 words, 2 of the girls' tapes and 2 of the boys' tapes could not be transcribed and analyzed because of recording difficulties.

The midadolescents were preoccupied by many of the concerns we noted in the monologues of the early adolescents, although there were certain shifts in emphasis. Little time was devoted to parents and siblings; animals were mentioned less frequently and almost never in great detail. Compared to the younger groups, the mid-adolescents demonstrated a much greater capacity to discuss a topic at length and in depth. Thoughtful commentaries on special interests, hobbies, and vacation trips were common. Competitive themes emerged somewhat less frequently and in more disguised forms than in the monologues of the early adolescents.

The midadolescents frequently discussed friends and acquaintances of both sexes but showed a noticeable trend toward private concerns. Many of the group were preoccupied with college and vocational plans. Introspective tendencies were marked, and irony appeared for the first time. A number of volunteers, both boys and girls, gave imaginative and entertaining descriptions of life at school and at home, poking fun at parents and teachers. Books, films, and other art forms were discussed. Boyfriends and girlfriends were mentioned but only briefly and in a matter-of-fact way.

The midadolescents directed a number of playful, aggressive remarks at the experimenters. These comments lacked the histrionic and more self-conscious flavor observed in the early adolescent group. Criticisms of the experimental procedure were more probing and sophisticated. Several volunteers showed a great deal of interest in the purposes of the study. Others expressed concern about their performance, but their remarks did not betray the same degree of anxiety and awkwardness shown by some of the early adolescents.

Adults

Twenty-three women and 23 men between the ages of 18 and 45 composed the adult group. We decided not to subdivide this group into subgroups spanning briefer age periods, assuming that changes in formal speech characteristics between 18 and 45 are too slow to be detected by our measures.

We already have described in Chapter 2 some of the demographic characteristics of this adult group. To summarize briefly, the men were volunteers from the U.S. Army and Air Force. Both officers and enlisted men were included, and they came from a variety of social and educational backgrounds. All had at least a high-school education and were screened carefully to rule out gross psychopathology. The women included employees and students working and studying at the University of Maryland Hospital. We had sufficient information about their personalities and work habits to allow us to exclude emotionally disturbed individuals from the experimental group.

All adult volunteers spoke the required minimum of 200 words. Several subjects complained about the difficulty in talking spontaneously with such little guidance, but no overt hostility, sarcasm, or playfulness were expressed.

The majority of the adult volunteers picked one topic and developed it during the entire 10-minute period. Some of the men gave short, autobiographical sketches, while others discussed army experiences and hobbies. Several delivered formal lectures in their areas of expertise. One volunteer, for example, chose military government as his topic. The women volunteers spoke about their school experiences, jobs, and personal lives. Although they mentioned parents, relatives, and friends, speakers of both sexes clearly were concerned more about themselves, their spouses or fiancés, and children, in that order.

Several adult males reminisced about past athletic triumphs, but competitive themes, at least in overt form, did not appear frequently in the monologues of this group. Discussion of animals and pets was completely absent. Some of the older volunteers, anticipating a tendency that was much more characteristic of the elderly subjects, presented a resumé of their past lives, a balance sheet of what had been accomplished, what still remained to be done, and which goals had to be abandoned. Some of the older armed-forces subjects expressed an attitude of resignation when discussing their past experiences and future prospects, a state of mind that was not at all evident among volunteers in the younger groups.

Senior Citizens

A group of 20 elderly subjects, 10 men and 10 women, completed our series of 6 groups. Aged 60–85, they were recruited from the Waxter Center for Senior Citizens, operated by the City of Baltimore. The volunteers were active, alert, and relatively free of crippling physical and psychological disorders. These senior citizens can be described as a group whose ability to cope with stress was influenced by the effects of normal aging but uncomplicated by severe pathology.

Drawn from a variety of socioeconomic and ethnic backgrounds, the volunteers were enthusiastic and highly cooperative. Many appeared grateful for the special attention they were receiving from representatives of a university medical center. The senior citizens considered themselves an unusual group. They were proud of their nationally-known center and took it for granted that they should participate in research projects. As a result, we had no difficulty in recruiting subjects for our study.

The senior citizens expressed the usual concerns of aging individuals during their 10-minute monologues, including medical problems, financial worries, children, and so on. The majority of the volunteers devoted most of their time to one of two themes: their activities at the Center and a recapitulation of the highlights of their lives. Many of these autobiographical accounts were philosophical and inspirational, particularly those produced by the women. The men talked less of other people in their lives and more of solitary activities.

As a group, the senior citizens spoke easily and well, although some found the procedure extremely tiring. Several made good-natured complaints about the experiment. No overt hostility was expressed, despite the fact that several volunteers had to wait almost two hours for their turn to speak. Compared to the younger groups, the elderly subjects were much more dependent upon routine in their daily lives. A number of them used the 10-minute period to describe a typical day in their lives, recalling the performance of the early schoolers.

Speech Patterns Associated with Age

Although we carefully segregated our volunteers by age, differences in rates of maturation undoubtedly accounted for a certain amount of overlap in their verbal performance. This is particularly likely for the younger subjects. Certain immature 12-year-olds undoubtedly were still functioning as latency children, whereas a few of the latter may have reached puberty already at the time we collected the speech samples.

A two-way, factorial analysis of variance was performed for age and sex in all 14 verbal categories.[2] The mean values and standard errors of means for the categories in which significant results were obtained are shown in Figures 3–1, 3–2, and 3–3.

Productivity, Rate, and Pauses

Figure 3–1 shows almost identical curves for productivity and rate; differences among age groups were found for both categories ($F = 8.59$, $df = 5/129$, $p < .01$); ($F = 10.39$, $df = 5/123$, $p < .01$). The early schoolers spoke significantly less and more slowly than subjects in all other age groups. Productivity and rate rose steadily through latency and adolescence, reaching their peak

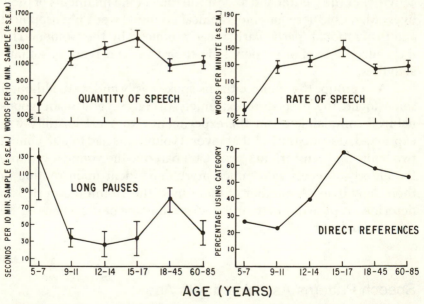

Figure 3–1. Use of Verbal Categories as a Function of Age (sample size ranges from 11 to 46).

in the midadolescent group. There was a moderate but significant decrease in both categories for the adults, followed by a leveling off among the elderly subjects. Not unexpectedly, we found an opposite pattern in the long-pauses category ($F = 2.55$, $df = 5/124$, $p < .05$). Of the 6 groups, the early schoolers had the highest mean and differed significantly from the early adolescents.

Our findings can be explained partly on the basis of neuroanatomical and neurophysiological factors. Efforts at thoughtful communication require retrieval of information in order to plan and encode new messages. Researchers have shown that this process retards the rate of speech in adults (Goldman-Eisler, 1968; Boomer, 1970). In general, the more complex the message, the slower the rate of speaking. We know that retrieval time, particularly for remote memories, decreases rapidly with age and is significantly higher among children than adults (Nelson, 1977b).

That the low productivity and speech rate of the early schoolers may have been due partly to information-processing factors is sup-

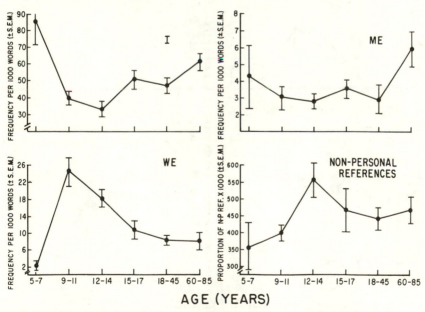

Figure 3–2. Use of Verbal Categories as a Function of Age (sample size ranges from 11 to 46).

ported by the following observation. The two early schoolers with the highest productivity and rate scores were those who told repetitive, precoded stories requiring little retrieval of information and almost no planning.

We cannot ignore the effect on productivity and rate of the young child's incompletely developed speech apparatus, particularly its neuromuscular control. Even the most rapid and productive early schoolers did not reach the mean values attained by any of the older groups.

We have been unable to discover in the literature reliable data comparing speaking rates of children of different ages, although investigators occasionally refer to lower utterance rates of very young children (Brown & Fraser, 1964). Most child psychiatrists and psychologists with whom we have discussed our findings have expressed surprise that early schoolers speak more slowly than older children. Some have attributed the results to the experimental setting, denying them any general validity. Only future investiga-

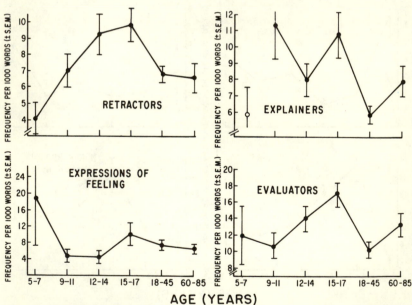

Figure 3–3. Use of Verbal Categories as a Function of Age (sample size ranges from 11 to 46).

tion will clarify this issue. We have noted that actors generally do speak more slowly when imitating the speech of children, a technique which renders their performance more believable to audiences.

The midadolescents' high productivity and rate suggest that information processing may reach its peak during this age period. Cognitive factors undoubtedly play a role, although anxiety may be a contributing factor. Many of the midadolescents were not only quick but witty, thoughtful, and creative. Compared to the less productive groups, increase in rapidity definitely was not accompanied by a decrease in the difficulty of the ideas discussed.

Our failure to find decreases in productivity and rate among the senior citizens is worthy of mention in view of published reports showing a significant decline in memory among the aged (Eisdorfer, 1978). It is true that most of the themes developed by the elderly subjects were stereotyped and unimaginative; it is possible that the senior citizens maintained a high level of productivity by relying upon repetitious, autobiographical accounts of low intellectual quality. Such a strategy on their part would have required only modest efforts at information retrieval and encoding.

Nonpersonal References, "I," and "We"

Considered together, these 3 categories provide us with a number of useful insights into developmental aspects of object relationships (see Figure 3–2). We can attribute significant findings ($F = 2.76$, $df = 5/129$, $p < .05$) in the nonpersonal references category mainly to low scores among the early schoolers and to frequent use among the early adolescents. In the *I* category, significant age differences ($F = 9.48$, $df = 5/129$, $p < .01$) are due largely to elevated values among the early schoolers and senior citizens and low scores among the latency children and early adolescents. Finally, significant differences in the *we* category ($F = 13.52$, $df = 5/129$, $p < .01$) can be attributed to elevated scores among the latency children and early adolescents. All other groups had relatively low scores, with the most depressed values found among the early schoolers.

Use of First-Person Pronouns: A Reflection of
Egocentric Speech in Early Schoolers

We can assume that the limited world of the early schooler is reflected verbally by the extensive use of herself, her immediate family, and a few friends as subjects of clauses. She has not yet developed sufficient detachment from her desires to be able to discuss events and relationships in which she does not play a central role. We can conclude from the extremely low *we* score that others still serve primarily as objects of gratification, rather than as genuine collaborators in work or play.

Our findings are congruent with Piaget's description of young children's spontaneous speech. The Swiss psychologist divided children's verbal productions into two categories: "egocentric" and "socialized." Egocentric speech is that in which the audience is disregarded. The child speaks for himself, rather than for his listener. Socialized speech, on the other hand, does take the point of view of the listener into account and includes actual exchanges of thoughts, remarks about the immediate situation, questions, criticisms, threats, and so on (Piaget, 1959).

Before the age of seven, according to Piaget, "the child is impelled, even when he is alone, to speak as he acts, to accompany his movements with a play of shouts and words" (p. 13). These egocentric monologues have no social purpose and occur with or without the presence of others. Piaget believes that much of the early schooler's social communication is expressed by means of gestures rather than words and that genuine socialized conversations do not begin before the age of seven. When children begin to speak in more socially adapted ways, egocentric speech gradually disappears.

Piaget analyzed children's spontaneous speech in the broader context of social relationships. He observed that small children do not work together often in groups. "Up until the age of about five, the child almost always works alone. From five to about seven-and-a-half, little groups of two are formed. . . . Finally, between seven and eight, the desire manifests itself to work with others" (1959, p. 41).

Although the first to describe egocentric speech in such detail, Piaget never really attributed important adaptive functions to it.

Vygotsky, on the other hand, noted that children used this form of verbalization most when "seeking and planning the solution of a problem" (Vygotsky, 1962, p. 16). Egocentic speech, in Vygotsky's view, does not atrophy and disappear at age seven but evolves into inner speech, the essential instrument of thought for older children and adults.

Grammatical Reflections of Group Formation in Latency and Adolescence

The scores of the fourth and fifth graders express a growing tendency toward group affiliation. Gesell, Ilg, & Ames (1956) have written of the ten-year-old that he "joins informal spontaneous groups and temporary fluid gangs. He tends to be tolerant rather than exclusive as to membership of these groups" (p. 39). Psychoanalytic clinicians have stressed the need of the latency child to develop group identifications. "The group for the latency child is a means of transition from the relationships with the parents to heterosexual objects and to society as a whole" (Bernstein, cited in Becker, 1965). Latency children's interests are, however, primarily home-bound. They enjoy doing many things with their parents, siblings, and neighborhood friends. To a greater extent than the early schoolers, they recognize that other people have lives and interests of their own; they can speak of happenings in which they did not participate. Unlike early schoolers, latency children are capable of genuine collaboration, a phenomenon that is reflected in a change in the relative frequency of occurrence of *I* and *We*. They also show increased capacity for detachment and objectivity by their greater use of nonpersonal references.[3]

Our discussion of group formation in latency-aged children is more accurate for boys than for girls. With the exception of a few girls who try to join boys' gangs, most girls in the 9–11 age group do not congregate in large units. They seem to prefer temporary, smaller groups of 2 to 4 members of their own sex. Psychoanalytic observers have attributed the lack of strong grouping tendencies among latency girls to a lesser need of peer support to strengthen sexual identity, as compared to boys of the same age (Kohen-Raz, 1971, p. 114).

Of the six groups, the early adolescents had the highest nonpersonal references score. They made frequent use of the impersonal "we," a consequence of their participation in large, ill-defined groups. Of this phenomenon, Gesell, Ilg, & Ames (1956) have written:

> It is at school and on the street and playground that [the 13-year-old's] sense of self experiences the powerful impact of the group, gang, team, and club. Here he encounters the flesh and blood images of his age mates. He glories in being one of them. [p. 144]

Helene Deutsch has described poignantly the young adolescent's attempt to cope with the anxiety resulting from the changes of puberty:

> The loss of childhood rights and gratifications; the uncertainty of the next refuge that is available to him for his "deserted" yet deeply dependent existence; the sense that now he has to prove himself as a grown-up member of society; and, finally, the ominous feeling of loneliness—all these serve to direct the young person away from the anxiety-laden "I" into the more secure "we" of a group of peers. . . . This is especially true during the earlier period of adolescence. [Deutsch 1967, p. 82]

The midadolescents were more preoccupied than the latency children and early adolescents with personal matters, as their thoughts turned to plans for college and career. Interest in group activities declined, animals and pets were mentioned infrequently, and current events were discussed in less detached ways. All these tendencies were reflected in a modest rise in the use of *I* and a decrease in nonpersonal references and *we* scores.

The trends noted in midadolescence continued in the verbal behavior of the adults and senior citizens, with no significant differences among the three groups emerging in any of the three categories under consideration. We wish to note that, taken together, the nonsignificant changes among the elderly—modest increases in nonpersonal references and *I*, accompanied by a small decrease in the use of *we*—do support the notion of social disengagement among senior citizens.

To summarize, changes in the use of *I* and *we* associated with increasing age reflect the often-described cycle of self-preoccupation in early childhood, group affiliation in latency and early adolescence, personal fulfillment through work and intimate relationships in later adolescence and adulthood, and gradual disengagement in old age. Since all subjects were strongly affiliated with institutions that absorbed much of their waking energies (private school, the armed forces, university, and a center for senior citizens), differences among the groups cannot be attributed to varying opportunities for collective experiences.

Group Participation and Restricted Linguistic Codes

Our finding that the frequency of occurrence of *I* and *we* is associated with group participation is supported by sociolinguistic research. Bernstein (quoted in Olim, 1970) has described two styles of verbal communication, involving both syntactic and lexical levels, which apparently are regulated by social relations. These codes are called "restricted" and "elaborated." Restricted codes are concrete, stereotyped, rigid, and contain few syntactic options. Their major purpose is to promote group solidarity; they arise "where the form of social relation is based upon closely shared identifications and common assumptions." Elaborated codes, on the other hand, are more differentiated, less predictable, and allow for more varied and complex expression of thought. Restricted linguistic codes supposedly are characteristic of the lower socioeconomic classes, while elaborated codes characterize the middle and upper classes. Of particular interest to us is Bernstein's comment (1970) that:

> A restricted code emerges where the culture or subculture raises the "We" above the "I." . . . Such codes will emerge . . . in such diverse groups as inmates of prisons, the age group of adolescents, army personnel, friends of long standing, or between husband and wife. . . . Restricted codes do not give rise to the verbally differentiated first person, "I," in communication.

Me

We found significant differences by age ($F = 2.65$, $df = 5/129$, $p< .05$) and sex ($F = 6.88$, df = $1/129$, $p < .01$) in this category. The age difference was due primarily to elevated scores among the early schoolers and senior citizens. Since the curve for *me* closely approximates that for *I*, we may be dealing with two aspects of the same phenomenon. The fact that women exceed men in their use of *me* but not of *I*, however, suggests that the two pronouns may have different psychological meanings. We believe that the use of *me* reflects a speaker's passivity, since this pronoun is almost always an object of a verb. This interpretation would account for the greater frequency of *me* in the samples of subjects in the typically more dependent age and sex groups.

Expressions of Feeling

Significant age differences in this category ($F = 2.53$, $df = 5/129$, $p < .05$) were due entirely to elevated scores among the early schoolers; they differed from all other age groups, with the exception of the midadolescents (see Figure 3–3).

We may picture the early schoolers as primarily concerned with the expression and gratification of wishes. According to Lewis (1977), they are "dominated by [the] immediate experience of a feeling [which] itself has an 'all or none' quality. [These children] cannot take distance from the feeling."

Most psychoanalyst observers agree that latency is characterized by a decrease in libidinal and aggressive drives and a strengthening of defenses. The latency child seeks gratification of desires through motor behavior rather than verbal expression (Bornstein, 1951; Kaplan, cited in Becker, 1965). The verbal style of latency is dominated by action, rather than feeling, words.

We now are faced with the problem of explaining why the surge of affectivity during early adolescence is not reflected by a high expressions of feeling score. It is likely that early adolescents keep a lid on their feelings because their fragile egos cannot permit extensive affective display without risking loss of control. In Anna Freud's words, "A quantitative increase in the drives takes place . . . [his] ego is not equipped to deal with these increased demands . . . [he] finds himself in inner disharmony, anxious, inhibited . . . and at variance with his environment" (1968). In a more descriptive vein, Gesell, Ilg & Ames (1956) have described the early adolescent as being "increasingly aware of his own feelings . . . but wanting to 'cover up' " (p. 155).

Not until midadolescence is the process of defensive reorganization sufficiently advanced to permit greater expression of feelings. The downward trend we found among the senior citizens may be due in part to the inevitable decrease in libidinal and aggressive drives accompanying advancing age.

Adolescent Criticism and the Use of Evaluators

Significant age differences in this category ($F = 2.72$, $df = 5/129$, $p < .05$) were due primarily to high frequencies of occurrence among the adolescents, particularly the midadolescents, who differed from both latency children and adults.

Since evaluators are concerned, to a great extent, with questions of right and wrong and good and bad, it is understandable that adolescents, who are preoccupied with the assessment of standards and codes of behavior, should have high scores in this category. We have referred already to the competitive themes developed by the adolescents in their monologues. These themes contained frequent criticism of people, styles, and institutions.

Adolescents characteristically oscillate between savage self-criticism and attacks against society. Deutsch (1967) has noted how many "project their own self-devaluation onto the outside world, thus trying to change themselves by way of changes in society" (pp. 84–85). The cognitive and emotional development necessary for objective criticism already has occurred in latency. The decrease in egocentricity, reflected in an ability to perceive external and intrapsychic events more realistically, permits the latency child to criticize, formulate attitudes, and pass judgments with a degree of detachment impossible among early schoolers (Kohen-Raz, 1971, p. 76).

Adolescent Impulsivity Reflected by
Verbal Retraction

We found significant differences in the retractors category for both age $(F = 3.92, df = 5/129, p < .01)$ and sex $(F = 5.26, df = 1/129, p < .05)$. Early schoolers made the least use of retractors. The scores then rose sharply through latency and early adolescence, peaked in midadolescence, and declined in the adult and elderly groups. Both adolescent groups differed significantly from the early schoolers.

Retraction suggests an ability to reconsider and to weigh alternatives; as such, it must be considered a sophisticated, adaptive mechanism. In a study of the language of elementary-school children, Loban (1963) noted that, "Those subjects most proficient with language are the ones who most frequently use language to express tentativeness." Vygotsky (1962) observed that second-grade children have not yet mastered the use of adversative conjuctives, so we should not be surprised that early schoolers scored low in this category.

Reconsideration, when carried to extremes, acquires a flavor of impulsivity and flightiness, characteristics generally associated with adolescence. Psychoanalysts have stressed the polarities and ambivalence of adolescence. Blos (1962) has noted how the adolescent's use of thinking as trial action is "constantly interfered with by the proclivity to action and acting out" (p. 124).

Intellectual Defense and the
Use of Explainers in Latency

This is another category in which the data showed significant age differences $(F = 4.92, df = 4/100, p < .01)$. We require a minimum of 800 words to score explainers reliably and too few early schoolers qualified to warrant inclusion of their age group in the statistical analysis.[4] Of the remaining 5 groups, the latency children and midadolescents had the highest mean values. The zig-zag curve seen in Figure 3–3 indicates that early adolescence is a period of regression with respect to causal thinking and expression.

We made no attempts to distinguish the different ways in which children and adolescents use connectives like "because." Piaget (cited in Corrigan, 1975) has shown that in the course of development, the same explanatory connectives express causal relationships of increasing conceptual complexity. We assume that the frequent use of explanatory expressions in spontaneous speech represents a predilection for rationalization as a defense, regardless of the quality of thinking demonstrated.

Clinicians have recognized for a long time that latency is the age period in which intellectual defenses predominate. Lewis (1977) has spoken of a postoedipal shift to an "obsessional organization." Another investigator has commented upon the scientific curiosity of children of latency age and their eagerness to perform laboratory experiments:

> Preadolescence is a more convenient period than early adolescence to take educational advantage of the student's desire to learn about nature, life, and his organismic problems. At early adolescence and puberty proper, the intensive pubertal changes may intensify egocentric tendencies and make the pupil less amenable to educational intervention. [Kohen-Raz, 1971, p. 154]

According to Piaget (1959), children do not talk spontaneously about causality among themselves before the age of seven or eight. Under the sway of egocentric thinking, the early schooler's logic is intuitive rather than deductive. He doesn't check propositions and makes use of personal schemes of analogy. "Causal explanation and logical justification . . . are still entirely identified with motivation," which leads to an anthropomorphic explanation of nature (p. 181).

Piaget noted in the speech of children aged 9 to 11 a very high frequency of occurrence of causative connectives, which he attributed to "a need for justification at all costs. The idea of chance is absent from the mentality of the [latency] child. . . . Every new perception is connected somehow or other with what immediately precedes it. . . . There is no 'why' that does not admit of an answer. . . . It is only very late [between 11 and 12] that he will say: 'One cannot know' " (Piaget, 1959, p. 147–148).

Confrontation through Direct References

A comparison of means revealed no significant differences in this category. Jaffe (1960b) has pointed out, however, that subjects' references to experimental procedures tend to be an all-or-none phenomenon, rather than one that most volunteers manifest to different degrees. We decided, therefore, to compare the various groups according to the percentage of subjects making one or more direct references.

A 2×6 χ^2 determined that there were significant differences among the 6 groups ($\chi^2 = 13.25$, $df = 5$, $p < .05$).[5] The lowest percentages of direct references were among the early schoolers and latency children, followed by a moderate increase in early adolescence. The percentage of subjects making direct references peaked in midadolescence, after which there was a modest decline among the adults that continued into old age.

Making direct references about the experiment or experimenter requires an ability to stand up to authority that generally is not found in young children. Oppositional tendencies, of course, are more characteristic of adolescents. We can attribute the decline in the use of direct references among the adults and senior citizens to increased conformity in the older age groups.

There were undoubtedly cognitive, developmental factors responsible for the low percentages of direct references in the younger age groups. Many of the items we scored as direct references in the adolescent and adult transcripts were descriptions of the volunteers' struggles to complete the experimental task. Such accounts involved a degree of self-observation that is unusual in childhood. Anna Freud (1965) has written, in this connection, that "introspection, which is a normal ego capacity in the adult, is not present in children . . . unless they are obsessional. . . . Their natural inquisitiveness is directed away from the inner to the outer world and usually does not turn in the opposite direction until puberty" (p. 221).

Sexual Differences in Verbal Behavior

We found significant differences between male and female subjects in three categories: (1) *Me* ($F = 6.88$, $df = 1/129$, $p < .01$); (2) retractors ($F = 5.26$, $df = 1/129$, $p < .05$); and (3) explainers ($F = 4.08$, $df = 1/100$, $p < .05$).

Me

In Chapter 2, we suggested that speakers use the personal pronoun, *me*, in intimate and receptive ways whereas *I* often functions as a more impersonal, active agent. If *me* does reflect in part a subject's passive strivings, it is not surprising that the female volunteers used this category more than the males. Sex differences did not emerge in adolescence, a possible consequence of increased female aggressiveness during this age period (Blos, 1958).

Retractors

Female subjects scored higher than the males in all age groups except for the early schoolers and the senior citizens. In a previous report comparing adult female and male speech patterns, we suggested that females' greater use of retractors seemed to confirm women's reputation for fickleness (Aronson & Weintraub, 1967a). The midadolescent girls scored higher in this category than all the impulse-ridden, deviant populations we have studied, including obsessive-compulsive neurotics; binge-eaters; and explosive, acting-out characters. We shall have more to say about the pathological forms of impulsivity in Chapter 4.

Explainers

The finding that female volunteers exceeded males in the use of *explainers* is unexpected and puzzling. If we focus on the defensive use of this category, we must attribute to women a greater tendency to rationalize. Although the differences in mean values between females and males were not large, they were present in all age groups. In interpreting the results, we may think of the excusing of one's thoughts and actions as being more characteristically female. Women, anxious to please and to avoid painful confrontation, smoothe the edges of controversy by explanation rather than defiance. We wish to note again that the sex differences, although consistent, are small; replication by additional studies is necessary to confirm or reject our findings.

Evaluators

Although data analysis revealed no significant sex differences, females of all groups, with the exception of early schoolers and senior citizens, exceeded the males in the use of evaluators. In an earlier publication, we reported that among adults, females scored significantly higher in this category (Aronson & Weintraub, 1967a). We attributed the difference to the greater need of women to be "good" and "proper." Many of the adult women were working in or training for helping-profession occupations.

Our data indicate that higher female mean values are present as early as latency and continue through adolescence and adulthood. Significant sex differences are obscured by their failure to become manifest among early schoolers and senior citizens. Is this an example of a sex difference that, according to Birdwhistell (1974), young children mature into and old people give up?

Expressions of Feeling

We found no sex differences in this category. Our findings are contrary to the results published by other investigators, who have reported significantly greater use of feeling words and expressions by women (Gleser, Gottschalk, & John, 1959; Hinchliffe, et al., 1977). For all our groups, excepting the early schoolers, female subjects did indeed exceed the males in the use of this category, but the differences did not even approach significance. We assume that variations in category construction and data collection account for the differences between our results and those of other investigators.

Integrating Patterns of Thought, Adaptation, and Speech

On the basis of the verbal data and themes developed by the volunteers in the different age groups, we now shall attempt to integrate patterns of thinking, acting, and speaking in a developmental sequence.

Early Schoolers

Small children lack the maturity and detachment necessary to understand the nature of experimental procedures. Even otherwise cooperative and obedient young subjects find speaking spontaneously for 10 minutes too long a time to maintain optimal performance. Nearly half of our group reacted to the stress of the procedure by withdrawing into total or near total silence. By not supplying even minimal amounts of support and encouragement, the experimenter became a frightening and intimidating figure; for some who did speak, he was a frustrating tormenter who deserved to be attacked.

For the most part, the early schoolers spoke slowly and deliberately. While we can attribute this phenomenon, in part, to the immaturity of the speech apparatus, other contributing factors undoubtedly included slowness in planning, retrieval time, and encoding. The more original the young volunteers tried to be, the more slowly they spoke.

The early schoolers developed themes reflecting a self-centered view of the world. Other than of themselves, they spoke only of family members and a few school and neighborhood friends. Their limited capacity for detachment and collaboration was indicated by the frequent use of *I* and by low *we* and nonpersonal references scores.

That the young subjects had not yet completely separated fantasy from reality was reflected by the bizarre and fantastic nature of several of the themes. Strong reactions to need frustration and regression induced by the unstructured setting were indicated by uninhibited playful and hostile behavior toward the experimenter. Compared to the other groups, the early schoolers freely expressed desires and feelings as shown by a high expressions of feeling score.

Although part of their syntactic repertory, the use of sophisticated coping mechanisms such as explaining and retraction was infrequent, suggesting that, under stress, more regressive adaptive maneuvers took precedence.

Latency Children

The widening world of latency children was reflected in significant changes in formal speech characteristics. No longer completely dependent upon parents, they were able to describe themselves as participants in groups of various kinds in school, neighborhood, and church. Others were seen not only as existing to serve children's needs but also as having desires of their own which children could help satisfy. This capacity to give as well as to receive undoubtedly accounted for the latency children's greater preoccupation with animals and pets.[6] This new way of relating to the world around them was demonstrated verbally by a dramatic decline in the use of *I* and an equally impressive increase in the use of *we*. The latency children's ability to observe people and events in more detached ways also was reflected in a rise in nonpersonal references.

The latency children exuded a sense of executive competence. Relatively free of acute conflict (Bornstein, 1951) and with an increased capacity to remember, plan, and articulate, they approached the experiment with vigor and confidence. They handled the task in a routine, businesslike way, and, if antagonism toward the experimenter was aroused occasionally, they were able to "create a realistic image of authoritative power on the one hand and obedience on the other" (Kohen-Raz, 1971, p. 19). These characteristics were reflected in greater verbal productivity, higher speech rate, fewer silences, and an avoidance of direct references.

The latency children's greater capacity for logical thinking, as well as their need to seek order in their environment, was mirrored in a high explainers score. They clearly were making use of their intellect to cope with the stress of the experimental procedure. A rise in retractors and a decline in expressions of feeling were further evidence that desire was being tamed by a broader range of sophisticated defenses.

Early Adolescents

Puberty ushers in a period of conflict and introspection. Reawakened sexual and aggressive drives were expressed by our subjects in various competitive themes. Early adolescents show a diminished capacity for social adaptation, and a number of our volunteers evidenced extreme self-conscious preoccupation during the experimental procedure. Their inclination for participation in poorly-defined peer groups of the same sex was revealed verbally in a low *I* and high *we* and non-personal references scores. Conflict between newly-fueled desires and increased demands of conscience was reflected thematically by numerous self-critical remarks; verbally, it was indicated by a rather high evaluators score. The early adolescents began to show a wider range of verbal defenses than subjects in the younger age groups, but their coping mechanisms were not developed sufficiently to allow a rich affective display.

Midadolescents

Although many of the concerns of puberty continued into mid-adolescence, a certain evolution was noticeable. Our subjects were more concerned with personal projects than peer-group activities. Their monologues were dominated by discussions of people and issues in relatively conflict-free areas. This transition was reflected by a drop in the use of *we* and nonpersonal references and a corresponding rise in the use of *I*. Expressions of feeling, so carefully monitored in early adolescence, occurred rather frequently, although not to the same extent as among the early schoolers. The midadolescents freely discussed their likes and dislikes but used an impressive array of defenses to cope with their emerging impulses. If their speech was rapid and their silences were relatively few, high retractors scores demonstrated that they were keeping all options open. Few had made choices with respect to future college or career. (The latency children, on the other hand, were much more definite about their future life's work, indicating that parental values had not yet been questioned seriously.)

Rapidity of discourse and frequent use of retractors contributed to the anxious, impulsive flavor of the midadolescents' speech. Explainers remained high in this age group, suggesting the continued extensive use of rationalization, while frequent occurrences of evaluators testified to the activity of an internalized critical agency.

Competitive urges were evident still, but their thrust was less pointed. We could see this in the midadolescents' use of direct references, which was characterized by polite, ironic criticism rather than the self-conscious hostility of the early adolescents or the regressive clowning of the early schoolers. Indeed, humor itself, in its ironic and sarcastic forms, became a potent weapon in the arsenal of the midadolescents.

As a group, the midadolescents expressed quickly and fluently many original and subtle ideas. Blos (1962) has called attention to this adolescent "concentration and dedication to the creative process of thought and imagery that is almost unknown before or after in the life of the average individual" (p. 126).

Adults

In adulthood, the struggle between impulse and defense has passed its peak. Expressions of feeling were down in our adult group, as were most defensive speech habits. Their need to deal with anxiety by a flight into words also decreased; productivity and rate were down and long pauses increased. The adults reflected in their monologues a certain calm after the adolescent storm. Overt competitiveness was unusual. In the experimental room, direct references were less apt to be hostile or sarcastic; a mild complaining tendency was more evident. The midadolescents' rapid, imaginative speech gave way to more deliberate, pedestrian language.

The adults placed personal concerns and projects above commitments to causes and ideas; their curiosity about issues and people rarely went beyond family and career. In their preoccupation with daily routine and moderate use of verbal defenses, the adults resembled the latency children to a certain extent. The principal differences between the two groups lay in the adults' greater capacity for confrontation, expressed by a higher direct references score, and a far lower investment in peer-group activities, reflected by a much lower *we* score. If the early schoolers and early adolescents showed signs of transition and conflict, the latency children and adults presented a picture of moderation, integration, and efficiency.

Senior Citizens

With our elderly subjects, we reach the end of the life cycle. Despite an average difference in age of over 40 years, the senior citizens' scores closely approximated those of the adults in almost all categories, indicating that once characteristic verbal styles are set in late adolescence, they change very slowly, if at all.

What we did observe in the speech samples of the senior citizens was an increase in self-preoccupation, reflected in numerous autobiographical themes. This was mirrored in increased *I* and decreased *we* scores. A rise in verbal productivity seemed to lend support to the stereotype of the garrulous, aged individual. We did not expect an increase in rate among the elderly; indeed, the increased productivity was traceable to the almost complete elimination of long pauses, a possible consequence of their extensive use of precoded material.

We wish to note a number of changes in the use of our categories by senior citizens, which, although not significant, are suggestive when considered together. We found that they used fewer qualifiers than the adults, which lent a flavor of rigidity to their monologues. Other characteristics attributed to the elderly, such as argumentativeness and opinionated behavior, were reflected in an increased use of explainers and evaluators. Hostile confrontation, on the other hand, was rare in the experimental room. Direct references were more apt to be in the nature of pleas for help.

Absence of Developmental Lag between the Sexes

We already have noted some published reports indicating female superiority in age-dependent language achievement. Certain themes, particularly those reflecting interpersonal sensitivity and heterosexual interest, appeared at an earlier age in the girls' monologues. Was there any evidence of a corresponding sexual lag in the use of the verbal categories? Our data do not support this notion, since no significant interaction effect between age and sex was found in any of the categories.

Interaction between Cognitive and
Emotional Factors in Language Development

Zig-zag and U-shaped curves associated with a number of our categories clearly indicate that cognitive, developmental factors alone
cannot account for the significant variations among the various age
groups. In language performance, as with other ego functions,
development along innately determined lines involves not only
anatomical and physiological processes but also "specifically pre-
scribed paths . . . [for] . . . the unfolding of drive action, impulses,
affects, reason, and morality" (Freud, 1965, p. 93). This point of
view has been summarized admirably by Kohen-Raz (1971):

> It would be erroneous to conclude that there is an antagonistic
> relationship between emotions and intellect or that the predomi-
> nance of each in the field of cognition is mutually exclusive. It would
> be more correct to say that there is a continuous interaction between
> intellectual and emotional functions which undergoes typical changes
> during childhood and adolescence. Actually, in order to give an
> over-all description of intellectual development at any stage, it is
> necessary to take into account not only the growing capacity to think
> logically but also the changing forms of interference of the irrational,
> egocentric, and magical elements of the mind with reality-adapted
> cognitive functions. [p. 42]

Sources of Misunderstanding in
Adult–Child Communication

Let us apply what we have learned to improving our communication
skills with children and adolescents. We fail to interpret children's
messages correctly, either through noncomprehension or misunderstanding. In cases of noncomprehension, we recognize that
we have not understood the child and make compensatory efforts to
clarify communication. Misunderstanding is more serious because
we do not realize that a message has not been transmitted or
received accurately.

All aspects of speech can be sources of noncomprehension or
misunderstanding. Phonological immaturity, which is reflected pri-

marily in errors of pronunciation, is a serious cause of noncomprehension but not of misinterpretation. We quickly realize that we are conversing with an immature speaker and will adjust by speaking slowly and using simplified syntax and vocabulary. Paralinguistic factors may lead to noncomprehension if we speak more quickly than the child can process our verbal signals. In such cases, we respond to the child's noncomprehension feedback and decrease the rapidity of our speech.

Syntactic immaturity can result easily in both noncomprehension and misunderstanding. Knowledge of age-related syntactic milestones are important here. We must realize that the use of grammatical structures implies a grasp of certain concepts. We cannot expect a child to use the past tense before he has understood the idea of the past. To avoid misunderstanding, we need only follow the child's lead. Since he will not use forms he doesn't understand, we are on safe ground if we limit our syntactic choices to those used by the child. Understanding a new form precedes the ability to use it actively by about six months. A child, therefore, may show understanding of a new concept although using an old form to express it. For example, a grasp of the idea of the past may be shown by the child's saying, "Yesterday, I see Daddy" (Moskowitz, 1978). In such a case, we can assume that the child will understand our use of the past tense.

Semantic immaturity presents very serious problems in communication and is perhaps the most common cause of misunderstanding between adults and children. This is because adults and children use the same words in different ways. To communicate effectively, the speaker and listener must have a similar set of mental associations to the word stimuli. Word association tests indicate that it is not until midadolescence that children understand most words in the same way as adults (Laffal, 1965). Before adolescence, children's associations to even neutral words are strongly colored by wishes and idiosyncratic experiences. Whereas the average adult in our society thinks of a table as an article of furniture, the child sees it as an object on which his mother serves him food. Failure to appreciate these distinctions can lead to subtle kinds of misunderstanding in adult–child conversations.

Finally, misunderstanding may result from a child not knowing how to participate in a conversation according to adult rules. This is more than lack of training and experience. A child or adolescent comes to an encounter with an adult with age-specific interests and expectations. We must expect children under the age of seven to use abbreviated grammatical forms and not to explain fully what they mean. This is because small children think that adults are omniscient and do not require explanations. We must realize that certain forms of humor are misunderstood by children. Sarcasm and irony should be used only with mature adolescents. Children under the age of 15 generally will interpret such attempts at humor as pure hostility. Adult metaphor is not understood before puberty and should be avoided with younger children. These are just a few of many examples of common sources of misunderstanding between adults and children. A thorough knowledge of language development will help us avoid many of them.

Summary

We have studied the effects of age and sex on the use of certain paralinguistic variables and the choice of grammatical structures. Our results show dramatic fluctuations in the use of most of our categories in childhood and early adolescence, followed by a leveling off in midadolescence and adulthood. Changes in frequency associated with increasing age clearly are not linear and cannot be explained entirely in terms of cognitive development. The data become more meaningful when age-specific shifts in the strength of drives and defenses are taken into account. With respect to sex, we find consistent differences in several categories for most age groups. We generally can associate both age and sex differences with patterns of observed nonverbal behavior.

Notes

1. Students of child and adolescent behavior are not consistent in their use of terms when categorizing developmental periods. The age period of 9 to 11, for example, is labeled "latency" by some and "preadolescent" by others. When comparing our

data with those of other investigators, we will be careful that the comparisons involve groups of children in identical age periods.

2. Where significant F-ratios indicated differences among age groups, Dunnett t tests were done to identify specific age groups between which significant differences occurred.

3. The latency child's greater use of nonpersonal references, compared to the early schoolers, may be due in part to cognitive, developmental factors, since the passive-with-agent-deleted construction is beyond the conceptual grasp of very young children.

4. The mean value of the 5 early schoolers who did speak the minimum 800 words is shown in Figure 3–3.

5. A subsequent 2×2 χ^2 with Yates Correction for continuity determined that significant differences exist between the latency children and the midadolescents ($\chi^2 = 5.10$, $df = 1$, $p > .05$), as well as between the 3 youngest and 3 oldest groups ($\chi^2 = 10.40$, $df = 1$, $p < .01$).

6. Blos sees the preadolescent girl's attachment to horses as a displacement from the oedipal father, as compared to her more maternal concern for dogs (1962, p. 70–71).

Chapter 4
Speech Patterns Associated with Deviant Behavior

In this chapter, we shall attempt to demonstrate, in a reasonably systematic way, what most clinicians assume: individuals sharing significant patterns of nonverbal behavior express these tendencies in their manner of speaking. Since we shall be concerned primarily with behavior that is both characteristic and deviant, our clinically derived categories, which have a slow rate of change, should be well suited for the task.

In studying the speech patterns of deviant populations, we shall try to go beyond the simple correlation of word and deed. We hope that we shall be able to demonstrate that knowledge of verbal style can be a basis for speculation about the meaning of behavior. Sophisticated psychoanalysts do, in fact, rely a great deal upon syntactic cues in making psychodynamic formulations and interpretive interventions. The importance of style in psychoanalytic work has been stressed by Edelson (1975), who has written, "The psychoanalyst's response to and use of strategies of syntax should . . . be as critical to his act of interpretation as his response to and use of semantic strategies" (p. 89).

A number of clinical investigators have tried to associate speech mannerisms with psychopathological states (Balkan & Masserman, 1940; Gottschalk, Gleser, & Hambidge, 1957; Lorenz & Cobb,

1952, 1953; Newman & Mather, 1938; Tucker & Rosenberg, 1975). Unfortunately, few researchers have been able to replicate the findings of others because of differences in category construction and sampling procedures (Andreasen & Pfohl, 1976). To a certain extent, these methodological difficulties have resulted from too great a reliance upon standard diagnostic criteria in defining patient groups. Such a practice makes the comparison of data gathered by different investigators extremely difficult for several reasons. First of all, regional style and tradition influence the definition of nosological variables. Secondly, patients' speech mannerisms often directly or indirectly affect the choice of diagnosis. This is particularly true of a disorder like mania, which we define partly on the basis of linguistic performance. Thirdly, certain diagnostic labels, like schizophrenia, are so broad that they are applied to individuals of widely differing styles of thought and action.

Forming groups on the basis of similarities in observable behavior rather than diagnostic labels does not do away entirely with the problem of contaminating variables, since we learn a good deal about a patient's comportment from his verbal account of it. There are, nevertheless, certain safeguards, particularly if we have available to us the observations of experimental subjects' nonverbal behavior.

To date, we have collected 10-minute free-speech samples from 6 groups of individuals sharing clinically significant patterns of nonverbal behavior. In a series of published reports, we have shown that speech samples of groups of impulsive, delusional, depressed, binge-eating, and compulsive subjects differed significantly from control volunteers in a number of our verbal categories. In general, the findings were consistent with patterns of psychological defense mechanisms attributed to these categories of patients by psychoanalyst observers (Weintraub & Aronson, 1964, 1965, 1967, 1969, 1974). Since we published these data, we have obtained verbal material from a group of female alcoholics.

We propose to compare the six deviant populations, both with the normal controls and among themselves, in order to determine whether verbal styles corresponding to observed patterns of nonverbal behavior exist. We used the method of data collection described in Chapter 2 to gather 10-minute free-speech samples from both control subjects and psychologically deviant volunteers. All 14 categories described in Chapter 2 were used in the verbal analysis:

1. Quantity of speech.
2. Rate of speech.
3. Long pauses.
4. Nonpersonal references.
5. I
6. We.
7. Me.
8. Negatives.
9. Qualifiers.
10. Retractors.
11. Direct references.
12. Explainers.
13. Expressions of feeling.
14. Evaluators.

Description of the Six
Psychologically Deviant Populations

Let us begin by summarizing the clinical behavior of the six deviant populations we shall compare. In all cases, psychiatric clinicians who did not participate in the scoring of the transcribed verbal material decided which volunteers met the criteria for inclusion in one of the deviant groups.

Impulsives

This group consisted of 17 psychiatric inpatients hospitalized at the University of Maryland Hospital. Although carrying a variety of diagnoses, all had in common a history of extremely impulsive behavior. Most were severe character disorders of various kinds. Several were diagnosed as schizophrenic, although none evidenced overt psychotic symptomatology during their hospitalizations. Since 2 of the 17 patients did not speak 200 words, we were able to use only 15 transcripts in our statistical analysis. The final group consisted of

10 women and 5 men between the ages of 18 and 45. All were from a middle-class background with at least a high-school education; approximately half had completed 1 or more years of college. In all cases, the patients had been admitted to the hospital following an impulsive act, usually of an attention-seeking, destructive kind. The impulsive behavior continued after hospitalization in the form of temper tantrums and self-destructive and assaultive acts, so that the ward personnel were able to confirm the historical data by direct observations. The patients attempted to undo the unfortunate consequences of their precipitate acts by apologizing for hostile outbursts, requesting help for self-inflicted injuries, and, in general, adopting a penitent attitude toward staff and fellow patients. During hospitalization, impulsive acts were observed to follow the frustration of desires. We can describe the behavioral pattern as follows: Refusal of a demand ⟶ impulsive act ⟶ attempt to undo the consequences of the impulsive act.

Before collecting the verbal samples, we made two predictions, based upon our familiarity with the pattern of impulsive behavior chosen for study. The first was that, since impulsive individuals tend to react to interpersonal stress by attempts to manipulate others, they would make direct appeals for help of the experimenter. This would result in their having significantly higher direct references scores than the control group. Second, since impulsive actions by their very nature are poorly conceived, they often are regretted. This leads to attempts to undo them, a tendency we predicted would be reflected in a significantly higher frequency of occurrence of retractors.

Delusionals

Like the impulsives, this group was composed entirely of University of Maryland Hospital psychiatric inpatients. Of 20 delusionals who volunteered for the study, 16, 9 women and 7 men, spoke the minimum 200 words. All subjects were over the age of 18 and from a middle-class background. Their educational achievement was comparable to that of the impulsives.

The delusional patients had the following behavioral pattern in common: prior to admission and during at least part of their hospitalization, they expressed in words and actions well-systemized delusions of either a persecutory or grandiose nature. The delusional patients did not demonstrate confusional symptomatology but were suspicious and intermittently withdrawn and occasionally had outbursts of hostility. Their admission to the hospital was precipitated at least in part by the overt expression of delusional ideas to family members, colleagues at work, or neighbors. All patients were voluntary admissions, although various amounts of persuasion were used by relatives, friends, and physicians to assure compliance with treatment plans.

The majority of the delusionals carried a diagnosis of paranoid schizophrenia, several were classified in one of the other schizophrenic subcategories, two were labeled "involutional melancholia," and one was considered to be a true paranoiac. No patients with known organic brain damage were included in the study.

In most cases, admission followed an acute behavioral disturbance. The patient, who had been functioning reasonably well at work and at home, characteristically complained that he was either being persecuted or was in danger of being harmed. Several delusional patients fled their immediate environment, others became assaultive or suicidal. Although the patients went through periods of withdrawal, they were, on the whole, a talkative group, eager to discuss their complaints and the reasons for their actions. Surprisingly, few delusionals refused to cooperate in the study, although several clearly misinterpreted its purposes.

From observations of previously hospitalized delusional patients and familiarity with defense mechanisms attributed to paranoid individuals by psychoanalytic clinicians, we predicted that subjects in this group would score significantly higher than the controls in direct references, negatives, explainers, evaluators, qualifiers and retractors. Our reasons for these predictions are as follows.

Direct references. Most delusional patients do not possess sufficient observing ego to speak for 10 minutes without attempting to involve the experimenter. The procedure itself provides strong stimulation for delusional elaboration. It seemed probable to us that a paranoid inpatient, faced with a stressful and unstructured experiment, might try to weave the new and strange experience into an existing delusional system. In the words of one clinical observer, "When he . . . feels himself under scrutiny, he proceeds as anyone else might by checking up and by putting events together that seem to belong together. . . . He unintentionally organizes others into a functional community, a group unified in their supposed reactions, attitudes, and plans with respect to him" (Cameron, 1943).

Negatives. If our assumption is correct that negatives reflect the defenses of negation and denial, we would expect a high score in this category. In his analysis of the Schreber case, Freud (1959c) emphasized the importance of psychotic denial in his formulation of the basic paranoid conflict. Cameron (1959), in his review of paranoid conditions, concluded, "Everyone seems to ascribe to denial and projection an abnormally large share in the defensive organization of paranoid personalities." Waelder (1951) attributed to denial a key role in paranoid delusional formation, one equal to that of repression in psychoneurotic symptom construction.

Explainers. Since rationalization is an essential element of delusional behavior, we predicted that explainers would appear frequently in the spontaneous speech of delusionals. A delusion represents, in part, an attempt by the paranoid to make sense of puzzling and frightening phenomena. To Freud (1959c), delusions were "attempts at explanation and cure." Other psychoanalyst observers similarly stressed the importance of rationalization in the thinking of paranoids (Cameron, 1959; Fenichel, 1945; Rapaport, 1951).

Evaluators. We assume that frequent expressions of judgment reflect the presence of an intimidating superego; therefore, delusionals should significantly exceed the controls in this category. Psychoanalytic writers are unanimous in their conviction that paranoids suffer from a tyrannical, punishing conscience. Freud (1959c) identified the delusional's persecutors as projected superego figures. Other observers have emphasized the formation of the paranoid superego from introjected parental figures (Glover, 1949).

Qualifiers and retractors. We predicted that the reluctance of the supposedly wary paranoid to take a definite position and stick to it would be reflected in high qualifiers and retractors scores.

Depressives

This group consisted of 23 women and 22 men, hospitalized on the University of Maryland psychiatric service. They were drawn from a larger group of 89 depressives, 44 of whom did not speak the minimum 200 words. All the patients were voluntary and from a socioeconomic and educational background similar to that of the impulsives and delusionals.

The depressives shared the following behavioral characteristics: for a period of time prior to admission, they expressed feelings of sadness, hopelessness, and helplessness. The depressives tended to blame themselves for their unhappiness; a number of them assumed responsibility for catastrophes with which they had had no connection. All patients in this group showed a decreased interest in work and family matters.

The depressives were free of confusional symptomatology and gross organic brain damage. Patients with overt schizophrenic thinking were excluded, but we made no attempt to achieve diagnostic purity in forming the group. In all cases, admission was brought about by a combination of depressive complaints and a decline in overall functioning. A number of patients had made suicidal gestures or threats.[1]

Compulsives

Seventeen patients having a pattern of ritualistic, compulsive behavior as a major symptom made up this group. Diagnostically, they were labeled as neurotic, character disorder, or borderline psychotic. At the time we collected their speech samples, the compulsives were being treated on both inpatient and outpatient services of university, Veterans' Administration, and state mental hygiene facilities in the Baltimore area. The patients varied in ego strength from very solid in certain outpatient neurotics to extremely fragile in a number of hospitalized, borderline personalities. In addition to their compulsive symptoms, some of the patients had classic obsessional character traits. The compulsive rituals included repetitive tightening of water faucets, continual checking of door locks, a need to point various articles in a certain direction, and so on. All patients were over the age of 18 and from a middle-class background. The group was composed of 11 men and 6 women. We needed a variety of clinical settings to provide us with enough compulsives for the study, confirming reports of their relative scarcity among psychiatric patients (Nemiah, 1967). All compulsives spoke the required 200 words.

In most cases, the compulsives sought help because of uncontrolled ritualistic behavior. The symptoms waxed and waned with the vicissitudes of life. The patients sought professional help when their control of key relationships was threatened. One young man was almost completely paralyzed by compulsive symptoms when his girlfriend challenged him to change his orderly ways. She kept him waiting for appointments, rearranged his furniture, and behaved in a provocatively untidy manner. The patient became increasingly angry and indecisive in almost all areas of his life. At the time he sought psychiatric help, he complained that he could not place the needle of his phonograph on a record in less than half an hour. Fearing that too firm a touch would damage the disc, he spent many frustrating minutes approaching the needle to the record and then withdrawing it.

Binge-Eaters

Our group of overeaters consisted of 18 adult women who were former patients of a University of Maryland weight-reduction clinic. The facility was not associated with the department of psychiatry and the binge-eaters did not consider themselves emotionally ill or in need of psychiatric treatment. The volunteers were from a lower-middle-class background, married, and most had at least one child. At the time of data collection, the binge-eaters' excess weight, compared with Metropolitan Life Insurance Company ideal weight tables, ranged from 6 percent to 164 percent, with a mean of 54.2 percent. All patients had taken the Minnesota Multiphasic Personality Inventory at the clinic; only those considered to be free of gross psychopathology were included in the study. The group, therefore, consisted of binge-eating women who wished to control their eating habits but lacked the willpower to do so. They were well-functioning members of their communities and were relatively free of disabling psychopathology.

We did not try to collect a group of binge-eaters with similar developmental histories. The subjects included women whose eating problems began in childhood, some who started to overeat as adolescents, and others whose weight problems did not become acute until after marriage or childbirth.

The volunteers had their binge-eating episodes following

minor incidents of rejection or abandonment. Several women, for example, reported overeating only when their husbands and children were away. After a period of internal conflict that varied in duration and intensity from subject to subject, the women rapidly consumed great quantities of food. The binges usually assuaged feelings of sadness and loneliness and were sometimes accompanied by excitement and elation. The women experienced regret and shame following their uncontrolled eating and attempted to undo the consequences of their impulsive behavior. They commonly made resolutions to diet and several of the volunteers had resorted to forced vomiting. We can summarize the binge-eaters' behavioral pattern as follows: rejection → craving for food → conflict → eating binge → shame and regret → attempt to undo consequences of binge. All subjects spoke the minimum 200 words.

Alcoholics

Our final deviant group consisted of 18 female alcoholics over the age of 18. They were all inpatients on an alcoholic rehabilitation unit at Springfield Hospital Center, Sykesville, Maryland. The group included both voluntary and committed patients. The alcoholic subjects all had chronic drinking problems that interfered with their ability to function in important areas of life. Often diagnosed as depressed as well as alcoholic, none was considered to be schizophrenic or organically damaged. At the time we collected the speech samples, the volunteers already had recovered from the acute drinking episodes that had brought them into the hospital. They were participating in a one-month experimental rehabilitation program, the purpose of which was to educate them about their drinking habits and to help them on the road to sobriety.

The group was quite heterogeneous with respect to drinking history and previous attempts at rehabilitation. What the women did have in common was hospitalization for an acute exacerbation of a chronic drinking problem and a willingness to participate in a program of rehabilitation. They were primarily from a lower-middle-class background and readily volunteered for the study. All spoke the minimum 200 words.

Control Subjects

Our 46 controls included 23 male members of the U. S. Army and Air Force and 23 female employees and students working and studying at the University of Maryland Medical Center. All 46 volunteers were between the ages of 18 and 45. We already have provided descriptive information about this group in Chapters 2 and 3.

Verbal Reflections of Deviant Behavior

A one-way analysis of variance was performed for the 7 groups in each of the 14 categories. Where significant F-ratios were found, Dunnett t tests were done to identify the source of significant differences between the deviant groups and the controls for all categories. The means, standard errors, and significant differences are shown in Tables 4–1 and 4–2.

Let us now consider briefly those categories in which significant differences emerged. We then shall attempt to construct speech patterns for the six deviant groups.

Quantity and Rate of Speech

We found that significant differences in these two categories were due primarily to low productivity, slow speech, and numerous silences among the depressives. That depressed patients often speak less and more slowly than other individuals is a well-known clinical fact. A certain subgroup of depressives, those we characterize as "agitated," may speak more rapidly than nondepressed individuals. When their clinical condition improves, both slow and agitated depressives approximate normal subjects in their productivity and rate (Aronson & Weintraub, 1967b). Our depressives' low productivity and rate indicates that the group contained more retarded than agitated patients. Actually, the scores do not reveal the true proportion of slow depressives, since only 45 of the original 89 volunteers spoke the required 200 words.

We were not surprised to discover that compulsives are talkative individuals. This fact is well known to experienced clinicians.

Table 4–1. Mean (S.E.M.) Verbal Scores for Control and Deviant Groups

Category	Controls	Impulsives	Delusionals	Depressives	Binge-Eaters	Compulsives	Alcoholics
Words	1104(65.8)	979.7(130.5)	961(117.0)	745.3(66.1)	985.4(112.5)	1132.2(107.0)	912.6(92.3)
Pauses	81.4(15.3)	138.8(41.7)	100.2(33.1)	195.8(24.2)	124.1(33.2)	92.0(35.9)	157.5(35.1)
Rate	124.9(5.3)	122.2(8.2)	113.1(4.2)	104.8(4.6)	121.3(6.6)	132.9(6.5)	116.3(6.9)
Nonpersonal References	440.1(32.7)	330.5(35.0)	362.9(41.7)	251.8(20.3)	323.4(34.9)	333.7(30.6)	363.9(44.1)
I	47.4(4.0)	77.6(7.8)	65.0(6.0)	83.9(4.5)	76.3(8.8)	72.3(6.5)	70.9(7.0)
We	8.1(1.3)	6.1(3.8)	6.7(3.3)	3.9(0.8)	7.9(2.2)	4.1(1.4)	7.1(2.5)
Me	3.0(0.4)	9.2(1.7)	9.0(1.5)	13.5(1.8)	4.8(1.2)	12.0(3.3)	9.6(1.7)
Direct References	1.4(0.3)	3.7(0.9)	2.9(0.6)	4.4(0.7)	2.4(0.6)	1.2(0.3)	2.0(0.5)
Qualifiers	10.6(1.1)	11.9(1.4)	13.5(2.5)	11.1(1.3)	11.5(1.6)	11.5(1.6)	10.2(1.5)
Retractors	6.6(0.5)	11.2(1.7)	8.1(1.6)	6.8(0.8)	10.9(1.0)	10.8(1.1)	7.4(0.9)
Feelings	7.4(1.0)	17.8(3.5)	10.1(1.7)	18.2(1.9)	18.0(2.3)	17.0(1.4)	14.4(2.5)
Evaluators	9.7(0.8)	15.1(2.1)	14.8(1.9)	18.7(2.0)	14.9(1.9)	14.0(0.9)	17.5(1.5)
Negatives	12.9(1.1)	29.6(3.3)	17.4(2.3)	20.6(2.4)	24.4(3.4)	20.6(1.8)	19.0(2.3)
Explainers	5.7(0.5)	8.0(1.5)	10.6(1.5)	5.6(0.9)	6.7(1.0)	8.9(0.8)	7.1(0.7)

Nemiah (1967), for example, wrote of the typical compulsive patient, "Any attempt to hurry him along, to cut him short, to switch to another topic is met by the patient's resistance and rigid adherence to his preconceived program of action."

Self-restraint, Dependence, and the Use of Direct References

The reader will recall that direct references are scored whenever the speaker makes comments about the experimenter or the experimental procedure. Depressives and impulsives scored highest in this category; the more stoic and detached compulsives had the

Table 4–2. Statistical Comparison of Deviant Groups with Normal Controls.

Category	F Values	Groups Showing Significant Differences from Controls
Quantity of Speech	2.95*	Depressives
Long Pauses	3.01†	Depressives
Rate of Speech	2.42*	Depressives
Nonpersonal References	4.73†	Depressives
I	6.54†	Impulsives, depressives, Binge-eaters, compulsives, and alcoholics
We	1.06	——
Me	7.18†	Depressives, compulsives, alcoholics
Direct References	4.51†	Depressives and impulsives
Qualifiers	< 1.00	——
Retractors	4.20†	Impulsives, compulsives, and binge-eaters
Expressions of Feeling	5.63†	Impulsives and depressives
Evaluators	4.07†	Depressives and alcoholics
Negatives	6.58†	Impulsives, depressives, compulsives, and binge-eaters
Explainers	4.23†	Delusionals and compulsives

*$p < .05$
†$p < .01$
$df = 6/168$ for categories 1–12; 6/118 for categories 13–14.

lowest mean value of the seven groups. Delusionals, although scoring higher than the controls, did not do so to a significant degree.

We observed that many of the impulsives had difficulty exercising the degree of self-restraint necessary to complete the experimental task. Several behaved as if they had not heard the instructions and tried to force the experimenter to break his silence. In the words of one observer of impulsive patients, "The object is sought primarily for need satisfaction" (Michaels, 1955). One woman began her monologue by shouting into the microphone, "Turn it off! Turn it off! You know, I—will you turn that thing off? Turn it off! You might think it's crazy but I hate to talk into these things." Another impulsive woman commented, "This is really a dirty trick. I can't think of a thing to say. . . . I think this is to see how good Dr. A. is at not showing any reactions whatsoever to any questions that I might put to him, whether I can make him crack a smile or not. . . . They get paid for listening to other people talk." We found these obvious attempts at manipulation to be typical of the impulsives' exasperating limit-testing behavior on the wards.

Depressives, of course, find the performance of any unstructured task to be extremely difficult. Almost half the volunteers were unable to speak the required 200 words. No other group we have tested, with the exception of kindergarten and first-grade children, had such a high percentage of non-talking volunteers. Many depressed patients asked the experimenter for help. The technicians who recorded the speech samples felt under great pressure to abandon their neutral role and offer assistance. The following excerpt from the transcript of a psychotically depressed woman was typical of the complaining, demanding behavior of patients in this group: "Doctor, I can't sit here. Please, you hear? I can't stand this no longer. Please, do something for me. Please, I know, but I can't stand it. . . . Please, somebody do something for me. Please, give me something."

The depressives' high direct references scores are consistent with clinical observations describing their relationships with others solely in terms of need gratification. In the words of one psychoanalytic writer, "The patients try to influence the persons around them to return their lost self-esteem. Frequently, they try to captivate their objects for affection" (Fenichel, 1945, p. 391). The technicians' responses to the depressives indicate the latter's extraordinary capacity to mobilize feelings of guilt and responsibility in those with whom they come in contact. This phenomenon has been noted and reported by other clinical investigators (Hinchliffe et al., 1977).

Although the delusionals did not use significantly more direct references than the controls, they occasionally expressed to the experimenter fears of being controlled, as in the following excerpt:

> *Male patient*: It is kind of frightening when you think about how electronics and machines are controlling a great deal of our lives and having such an influence. It's somewhat dehumanizing. I can imagine whoever is listening to this playback shifting around restlessly from boredom.

Detachment and Objectivity as Reflected in the Use of Nonpersonal References and "I"

We attribute significant differences in these two categories to a personal style of speaking among depressives, impulsives, and binge-eaters. Since the normal volunteers scored at the extreme end in both categories, we may be dealing with a nonspecific effect related to psychological deviancy. The development of a sense of objectivity toward oneself and the environment must be counted as one of the criteria of mental health. In a study comparing the speech of hospitalized psychotic inpatients with normal controls, Gottschalk, Gleser, & Hambidge (1957) found that the patient group made more self-references and fewer group references. Natale, Dahlberg, & Jaffe (1978) reported a negative association between the use of personal references and improvement in psychotherapy. Compared to normal subjects, neurotic patients have been found to use the pronoun *I* more frequently (Lorenz & Cobb, 1953).

The depressives' frequent use of *I* and other personal references appeared to be symptomatic of extreme self-preoccupation. Most of the group were unable to take distance, even temporarily, from their morbid concerns; they succeeded only in uttering monotonous, repetitive complaints. The technicians who recorded the speech samples, the typists who transcribed the tapes, and the judges who scored the protocols all reported feelings of tedium, irritation, and sadness during their work on the project. The following example, taken from the transcript of a middle-aged woman, conveys something of the flavor of depressive speech: "Oh, I'm so cold in here. Can't you take me out of here? Now, you know this is awful. Bring you in here and let you stay in here. What do I know? Wonder if I can get out of here." Freud (1959b) observed that the "trait of insistent talking about himself and pleasure in the consequent exposure of himself predominates in the melancholiac."

We can interpret the impulsives' frequent use of *I* as a confirmation of their extreme self-preoccupation. The fact that they did not differ significantly from the controls in their use of direct references suggests to us a capacity for detachment from people who are not available for need gratification.

The binge-eaters' scores in these two categories were close to those of the depressives, although not quite so extreme. They spoke primarily about concrete, personal problems, such as weight-reduction, family issues, and routine, daily activities. Compared to delusionals and compulsives, the binge-eaters spoke hardly at all about topics of general interest. Other investigators have noted this tendency toward concreteness and self-preoccupation among individuals with eating problems (Friedman, 1959; Werkman & Greenberg, 1967).

Passivity among Depressives and Compulsives Mirrored in Use of "Me"

We can see in Table 4–1 that most of the variance in this category is due to low scores among controls and binge-eaters and high frequencies among depressives and compulsives. The depressives saw themselves as being acted upon, a reflection of their passive attitude toward their environment. At times their passive use of *me* was quite obvious, as in the following excerpt from the monologue of a middle-aged man:

> Got four grandchildren that I wanted to look up to *me*. But they seem to see right through *me*. And they don't have any more respect for *me* than the other ones did. My son has no respect at all. Talks to *me* worse than to his casual acquaintances. Even though I—he feels that coming into the hospital would make *me* see his way in a different light.

The reader will note that the passive use of *me*, which appears five times in this quotation, is emphasized in the last sentence by a sudden shift from an active to an impersonal, grammatical construction; the patient shifted responsibility for a belief from himself to his son.

The compulsives' frequent use of impersonal, passive syntactic structures is in accordance with common clinical observation. They tend to see themselves as being acted upon rather than as responsible for their own thoughts and actions. The compulsive doesn't do things; they happen. He doesn't think; thoughts come to him. We offer the following quotations, taken from the transcripts of two compulsive patients, to illustrate the use of *me* by those who see themselves buffeted by forces beyond their control. We can observe that the two compulsives describe themselves as passively experiencing both conflict and satisfaction.

> Woman: The fight, I believe, is going inside of me . . . as if something in me were just wringing . . . just squeezing me on the inside. . . . I'm going to try . . . no matter how the compulsion drives me . . . to let my normal feelings rule me.
>
> Man: School for me has become one of the main hinges of my life . . . biology interests me. . . . Sometimes, the classroom cramps my style . . . things are really quite comfortable for me at home, perhaps too comfortable.

Retractors as Indicators of Impulsivity

We see that significant findings in this category were due to high frequencies among impulsives, binge-eaters, and compulsives. The lowest mean values were found among the controls and depressives.

The impulsives' high retractors score confirmed our prediction and accurately reflected their nonverbal behavior. We cannot be certain, of course, that retraction is characteristic of all impulsive actions. It is possible, although unlikely, that individuals whose impulsivity is ego-syntonic do not use undoing mechanisms. Our groups of impulsives were, after all, guilt-ridden, psychiatric inpatients. Frosch & Wortis (1954) have emphasized this quality of impulsive behavior, which leads to "self-castigation" and "self-reproach." The following quotations from the monologues of two impulsive women indicate how subjects from this group used retractors.

> *First woman:* I don't go in too much for alcoholic beverages. The crew I hang around with at parties and all, they usually get a little smashed, *but* I don't do that too much. I used to, it was a big thing when I was younger *but* now it's nothing. I've known a few dope addicts, *not addicts actually*. I never really did know anyone that got hooked on it. I've never taken any dope, *though*, *although* I've known quite a few people that have.
>
> *Second woman:* I realize that for the time being I am considered incompetent *although* I don't really feel that incompetent anymore. *But* to a lot of people anything I say—my views and outlooks—would just be considered the raving of a mad woman. *But* that doesn't bother me too much when I'm normal, when I'm feeling, *but* I always felt that. I don't think I was terribly maladjusted before my marriage *but* there are a few things, when I think about it, that could have been better.

If we think of binge-eaters as a special category of impulsives, their frequent use of retractors is understandable. We have noted already their attempts to undo the effects of their binges, a phenomenon reported by Stunkard (1959). The binge-eaters frequently blurted out remarks that they quickly retracted, particularly when they discussed sensitive subjects like weight-reduction, as in the following example:

> I've been heavy, I think, all my life, as long as I can remember. And I didn't like it very much, *but* I never did too much about it, and I don't know if it's too late now or not. *But* I think I would feel better mentally and physically both if I would lose some weight . . . my husband . . . would like it if I would lose some weight . . . *but* I tried—*but* I didn't—I'm not successful at it. I have a little boy and—he doesn't mind me the way I am—*I guess*—*but* my older children do.

If we think of retraction as a verbal expression of the defense mechanism of undoing, the compulsives' elevated score is congruent with clinical reports. Psychoanalyst observers agree that undoing is a key mechanism in the development of obsessional thinking and compulsive behavior. Freud (1959a) described the use of undoing as an attempt to cancel a previous, forbidden action.

Our prediction that delusionals would exceed significantly the controls in this category was not confirmed. Paranoids may have difficulty sticking to commitments only during the early stages of their illness. Once the delusions have become fixed, retraction tendencies apparently diminish in strength. Federn (1952) noted a quality of "false certainty" in the paranoid's delusional system.

Justification among the "Intellectualizing" Groups

Delusionals and compulsives made the greatest use of explainers. We already have given our reasons for predicting high scores in this category for the delusionals. The compulsives' use of reasoning for defensive purposes is well known. Rapaport (1951) described them as one of the "intellectualizing groups." According to Nemiah (1967), the compulsive "relies heavily on rational argument and talks in highly intellectual and intellectualized terms about the subject matter." The compulsives' frequent use of explainers is, in part, an attempt to justify magical thinking and irrational behavior.

Affective Display and Expressions of Feeling

Depressives and impulsives had the highest expressions of feeling scores; controls, delusionals, and compulsives had the lowest. That our depressives made the most use of feeling words seems natural for victims of an affective disorder. Clinicians will not be surprised to learn, however, that few patients in this group actually described themselves as having feelings of sadness. They were more likely to make concrete references to their likes, dislikes, hopes, and desires, as well as to various physical sensations. Just as the depressive often cannot cry real tears, he seemingly lacks the ability to appreciate and convey his innermost feelings to others. What we heard was a tiresome, repetitive recitation of complaints and demands, with the accompanying message that nobody could do anything about them. Asking for help but not accepting it makes the depressive frustrating and demoralizing to those around him.

Impulsives resembled the kindergarten and first-grade children, described in Chapter 2, in the uninhibited way they expressed their likes and dislikes, fears, and joys. The inability of impulsives to contain their feelings is one of the few points upon which investigators of these patients agree (Michaels, 1959). We offer the following brief excerpts, taken from the transcripts of two female impulsives, to demonstrate the direct, untamed expressions of feeling we found in no other adult group: (first woman) "I hate tape recorders. I despise them." (second woman) "I can't stand two of my sisters. I love my brother and one sister very, very much. I love my father." We can consider the impulsive act itself as an explosive expression of feeling. Impulsives lack skill in the verbal modulation of affective responses, and our group gave ample evidence of raw emotional outbursts in the hospital.

Although the compulsives scored lower than most of the other deviant groups, they used more expressions of feeling than the controls. How can we reconcile this finding with their clinical reputation as impersonal and detached? We believe that this apparent discrepancy arises from two sources. First of all, clinicians have not always distinguished neurosis from character disorder when describing obsessive-compulsive patients. Lack of expressiveness and extreme detachment are personality traits, and not all patients in this group had compulsive characters. Secondly, our patient group although sharing a pattern of compulsive symptomatology, contained individuals of different degrees of decompensation. Some were hospitalized, borderline individuals; others had clinically significant depressive symptoms in addition to their ritualistic behavior.

Negative Speech in the Service of Oppositional Behavior

All deviant populations exceeded the controls in the use of negatives, the depressives and impulsives to a significant degree. We believe that it is unrealistic to interpret these findings solely in terms of denial and negation. While these mechanisms undoubtedly are reflected by the use of negatives, other, more superficial aspects of thinking and behavior may be equally important. We believe, for example, that oppositional tendencies, often expressed clinically by withdrawal and rebelliousness, are associated with the use of negatives. Looking at the data from this broader perspective, we can report that the impulsives were by far the most resistant of the deviant populations. In ways we have described already, they were least cooperative with the hospital staff and complained most about the experimental procedure. The following excerpts give evidence of the impulsives' use of negatives to express oppositional behavior:

> Woman: I have *no* interest in anything. I have *no* interest in any friends. I *don't* care to see any friends. I have *no* desire to have cards, receive cards. When I receive flowers, I have *no* interest.
> Man: I really *can't* talk in these things. I *can't* talk to you and I *couldn't* talk to Dr. B. and I *can't* talk to the analyst I was seeing."

Superego Activity and the
Expression of Value Judgments

Since evaluators refer to concerns about morality and propriety, we were not surprised to find that the six deviant groups exceeded the controls in this category. The demands of conscience undoubtedly weighed heavily on members of all deviant populations. As we might expect, the depressives scored highest, differing significantly from the controls. Psychoanalytic formulations of depressive symptomatology always have emphasized the activity of a cruel superego as a sadistic tormenter of the self (Fenichel, 1945) and as an inflexible tyrant requiring the atonement of a penitent ego (Rado, 1928).

The volunteers' use of evaluators probably reflected a variety of conscious and unconscious phenomena. The category is extremely broad and combines references to matters of morality, ethics, and convenience. We undoubtedly would attain greater powers of discrimination were we to divide evaluators into several subcategories. In Chapter 8, we shall return to this question.

Speech Patterns of Deviant Populations

Let us now try to construct speech patterns for the psychologically deviant populations. For each group, we shall compare verbal with nonverbal behavior and, where appropriate, with underlying mechanisms of defense.[2]

Impulsives

Compared to the controls, the impulsives scored high in the following categories: *I*, expressions of feeling, direct references, negatives, and retractors. Both predictions we made prior to the collection of the samples were confirmed. Let us compare these verbal characteristics with the striking nonverbal behavioral pattern shared by members of this group.

The "impulsive episode" typically began with the frustration of a desire. The patients and hospital staff described the ensuing affective response as a mixture of rage and anxiety. Verbally, we can associate this reaction with a high expressions of feeling score. The impulsives' refusal to accept reasonable limits, combined perhaps with attempts to deny dysphoric feelings, was reflected by a high frequency of negatives. Their manipulation of the human environment in attempts to obtain gratification and reassurance was translated into a significant use of direct references. We assume that the guilt and shame aroused by the immature outburst led to attempts at atonement, a maneuver reflected in a high retractors score. Self-centered concern with the satisfaction of personal desires was reflected in the frequent use of *I*.

To summarize, we speculated that the impulsives could not tolerate the affective storm resulting from the frustration of their desires. Their rage was denied and desperate attempts to enlist the aid of others was followed by guilt and attempts to undo. Since the impulsive's symptomatic behavior is so clear, we shall attempt a

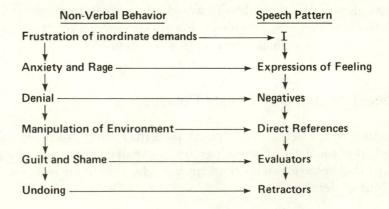

direct comparison of speaking and nonverbal patterns of behavior, as shown in the following diagram.

In his monograph on episodic behavioral disorders, Monroe (1970) has proposed a modification of this scheme. While agreeing that some denial probably precedes attempts at manipulation, most of it, according to Monroe, occurs after completion of the guilt-arousing behavior. The impulsives' attempts to assuage feelings of guilt are said to require the simultaneous mobilization of the defenses of denial, undoing, and rationalization. We have no quarrel with Monroe's formulation, except to point out that our impulsives did not exceed the controls significantly in their use of explainers, the verbal expression of rationalization.

Delusionals

Only one of our six predictions was confirmed for the patients of this group. The delusionals scored significantly higher than the controls in their use of explainers. In the five categories in which our hypotheses were not confirmed, differences in mean values between delusionals and controls were all in the predicted direction. The direction of differences of means was, therefore, correctly predicted in all six categories ($\chi^2 = 6.0$, $df = 1$, $p < .01$).

The delusionals emerged as the most "intellectualizing" group. Compared with the other deviant populations, they were somewhat less self-preoccupied and passive (moderate use of *I* and *me*), reasonably positive in their approach to the experiment (moderate use of negatives), and not given to affective display or quick judgments (moderate incidence of expressions of feeling and evaluators).

Since delusionals do not show extensive syntactic aberrations, some researchers have described them as having no distinctive verbal style (Mirin, 1955; Maher, 1972). Other investigators, however, have reported grammatical differences between paranoids and normal subjects. Lorenz & Cobb (1954), for example, after observing that their group of paranoid schizophrenics did not "stand out so clearly with specific language habit," stated that the patients used fewer pronouns, had an *I* frequency within normal range, and had a predilection for the pronoun, "he." In a more detailed report, Lorenz (1955) observed that paranoids often give preference to "impersonal constructions," make frequent use of "qualifications" and "negations," use the "indefinite" in preference to "I," and show a "passive orientation . . . by the frequent use of the passive voice and other verb constructions suggestive of passivity." According to Lorenz, paranoids also made extensive use of reflexive pronouns like "myself." Although certain of her data are congruent with our results, comparisons are difficult because of differences in data-gathering techniques and patient selection.

Studying Schizophrenic Bizarreness

Before completing our discussion of delusional speech, we wish to make some comments about problems inherent in the investigation of schizophrenic verbal behavior. We decided not to include a group of schizophrenics among our deviant populations for two reasons. First of all, the label "schizophrenia" includes such a wide variety of behaviors that there may be no one pattern that distinguishes the entire group from normal individuals or from other deviant groups. Secondly, many of the classic symptoms of the disorder, particularly as described by Bleuler, are based upon verbal peculiarities. In choosing delusional patients, we selected a schizophrenic subgroup on the basis of criteria that had little to do with speech variables.

We wish to propose the following strategy as a way of selecting a schizophrenic group on the basis of nonverbal criteria. Although no single nonverbal pattern characterizes all schizophrenics, we believe that "bizarreness" probably comes as close as any to the essence of the clinical picture. With the help of silent videotapes, judges could choose schizophrenic subjects whose posture, gait, gestures, and the like were considered to be bizarre. Speech samples could be collected from such a group and compared with monologues from a group of subjects whose nonverbal behavior had been judged to be free of bizarre qualities.

Although investigators have published reports of schizophrenic speech, the verbal reflections of bizarreness have never been identified and described clearly. Certain researchers have raised the interesting hypothesis that the verbal counterpart of bizarre behavior may be the transmission of incomprehensible messages in grammatically intact form (Steingart & Freedman, 1976). When both semantic and syntactic aspects of speech are disorganized, the effect is more apt to be one of confusion rather than bizarreness. Children are able to speak nonsense without appearing bizzare because they demonstrate immaturity in both form and content. Entertainers can create nonbizarre, comic impressions by speaking nonsense in syntactically correct language, but this probably is accomplished by a combination of appropriate gestures, ordinary rather than esoteric thematic content, and a clever sprinkling of puns. To put matters another way, a bizarre or humorous effect is produced when recognition is present in the absence of understanding. When both are absent, the impression conveyed is one of confusion in adults and immaturity in children.

Depressives

Subjects in this group scored significantly higher than the controls in the following categories: negatives, expressions of feeling, direct references, long pauses, *I*, and *me*. Their scores were significantly lower for quantity of speech, rate of speech, and nonpersonal references.

Before attempting to interpret the data, let us review the pattern of depressed behavior shown by our patients. Following loss or rejection, the depressives began to complain to family and friends in a sad and hopeless manner. They showed decreased interest in work and family activities, which at times seriously affected their ability to function in these areas. The depessives generally manifested retardation of movement, although a number of them were agitated. Their complaints to loved ones were couched in terms of self-blame and shame. Many made suicide attempts.

Let us now try to associate the depessives' nonverbal behavior with their pattern of speaking. Their state of psychomotor retardation and withdrawal were reflected, of course, in decreased speech productivity and rate as well as in long and frequent silences. Although Arieti (1959) has attributed defensive functions to both slow and agitated speech, a psychophysiological basis for these phenomena seems more likely. In some way, as yet poorly understood, information processing is impaired in the depressive syndrome, leading to the characteristic symptomatic verbal behavior.

Of our six deviant groups, the depressives were clearly the most disturbed and regressed. Unstructured interviews are known to be extremely stressful for psychotic patients, and this may have accounted in part for the depressives' low productivity.

Self-preoccupation and loss of interest in work and family were expressed verbally by a high *I* and a low nonpersonal references score. The depressives' regression to a state of pleading, passive helplessness was translated into a high frequency of *me* and direct references. Their complaints about dysphoric feelings and the vicissitudes of life were mirrored in a high expressions of feeling score. A plethora of negative judgments about these same complaints resulted in numerous evaluators. Finally, their reluctant attitude toward participation in activities, including the experimental procedure, accounted for the high negatives score.

From a psychodynamic point of view, we can associate the frequent use of negatives with the denial of a lost object; the various changes in productivity and rate with attempts at oral introjection; a high evaluators score with ensuing guilt; and the frequent use of direct references with attempts to gain reassurance from external objects.

If we compare our data with those of other inestigators, we observe certain similarities. In a detailed clinical report, Newman & Mather (1938) noted that classical depressives spoke slowly, paused frequently, used simple grammatical structures, and showed little variety in their verbal responses. A team of British investigators (Hinchliffe, Lancashire, & Roberts, 1971) used a modification of our procedure to compare the verbal behavior of a group of middle-class, depressed psychiatric inpatients with that of a group of normal controls. They reported significant differences in rate of speech, negatives, and expressions of feeling in the same direction as our findings. We believe it is particularly noteworthy that the British study replicated a number of our findings with subjects drawn from a different national and cultural background.

Andreasen & Pfohl (1976), in a study comparing manic and depressive speech samples, confirmed our finding that depressives are unusually high in the use of "personal" references. In a study comparing nonparanoid schizophrenic, depressive, and paranoid speech, Steingart & Freedman (1972) reported that paranoids used the fewest self-references in the subjective case, while schizophrenics used the most. According to the authors, extensive self-reference use indicates narcissistic content and a low degree of self–object differentiation. Although there may be some validity to their claim, we have failed to find in our studies of children and deviant adults any consistent relationship between the use of *I* and immature or psychotic behavior. We believe that the choice of *I* is determined by a number of factors, both developmental and psychological, and is not simply a reflection of the degree of self–object differentiation.

Compulsives

We found significant differences between the compulsives and the controls in the following categories: *I*, *me*, negatives, explainers, and retractors. How can we weave these results into a verbal pattern that corresponds to the symptomatic behavior of the patients in this group?

The magical world of the compulsive, in which words and gestures are invested with enormous power, is passively contemplated by the self-preoccupied patient, a clinical state that was reflected verbally by a high frequency of *I* and *me*. Passive pseudo-compliance and denial of reality "at the point where it opposes the patient's wishes" (Fenichel, 1945) combined to produce a high negatives score. The compulsives' undoing of forbidden thoughts and actions accounted for their high retractors score, whereas their need to make sense of irrational thoughts and actions resulted in the frequent use of explainers.

How do our findings compare with those of other students of verbal behavior? Several clinical observers have commented upon the speech patterns of compulsive patients. Since these authors did not indicate whether compulsive neurotics or characters were being discussed, we cannot be sure that their subjects were similar to ours. Lorenz & Cobb (1954) compared speech samples of "obsessives" with those of manics, hysterics, paranoid schizophrenics, and normal control subjects; in their study, 1000 word samples were taken from "non-directive, recorded interviews." Among other findings, the authors reported the extensive use of *I* and the frequent occurrence of passive verb constructions and adverbs. In a later publication, Lorenz (1955) offered the following impressions of compulsive speech:

> One can detect a mental set toward judgment and evaluation . . . a characteristic device of the obsessive-compulsive is the use of terms of quantity, comparison and degree . . . frequent use of negation linked with subsequent positive statement . . . frequent use of substantives denoting concepts and abstractions rather than specific feelings or objects . . . the frequent use of the disjunctives "or," "if," and "but."

Lorenz noted a number of other interesting and important compulsive speech habits, but they are not directly comparable to our verbal categories. In general, where comparisons are possible, there are few differences between her findings and ours.

The compulsives' predilection for connectives of various kinds may reflect their fear of being dominated. By skillfully using conjunctions, they can manage never to finish sentences, thus controlling conversations without fear of interruption.

Binge-Eaters

Of the six deviant groups we studied, the binge-eating women were the only nonpatients. We cannot, therefore, attribute verbal differences between them and the controls to patient status.[3] The binge-eaters scored significantly higher in three categories: negatives, *I*, and retractors. In addition, the obese volunteers came very close to using significantly more expressions of feeling and fewer nonpersonal references.

The reader surely has noted a number of similarities in the speech patterns of the impulsives, depressives, and binge-eaters. All three "oral" groups scored high in three categories: *I*, negatives, and expressions of feeling, the verbal indicators of self-preoccupation, denial, and immoderate affective display.

A number of reports in the literature link depression, obesity, and impulsivity. Certain investigators have emphasized the low frustration tolerance of obese patients (Bruch, 1943; Schick, 1947; Werkman & Greenberg, 1967). Fenichel (1945) considered the psychodynamics of impulsives and overeaters similar enough to have characterized the latter as "impulse neurotics."

Obese individuals are often said to overeat in order to ward off feelings of depression. Werkman & Greenberg (1967), for example, characterized obesity as a mask for depression. Depression occasionally may be precipitated by dieting (Rascovsky, de Rascovsky, & Schlossberg, 1950).

Alcoholics

Our alcoholic women scored significantly higher than the controls in three categories: *I*, *me*, and evaluators. Their expressions of feeling and negatives scores, although falling short of significance, also exceeded those of the normal group. It is clear that these results point in the direction of another "oral" syndrome. The elevated *I* and *me* scores reflected a certain passive self-centeredness. We assume that the frequent use of feeling expressions indicated a potential for depressive decompensation, unfortunately too often realized in the histories of these unhappy women. Finally, the alcoholics' high evaluators score suggested the presence of a rigid superego, a finding noted in the other "oral" patient groups, with the exception of the better-adjusted binge-eaters.

The role of specific personality variables in the etiology of alcoholism is controversial among knowledgeable clinicians. The current wisdom is not to assume an association between pathological drinking and any cluster of personality traits that can be designated as an "alcoholic personality." Clinicians, of course, have referred in the past to the alcoholic's frequent use of denial and to his depressive and paranoid tendencies (Chafetz, 1967).

The alcoholic women were heterogeneous with respect to diagnosis and drinking habits. Other than drinking, all they had in common was their willingness to participate in a rehabilitation program. We should not be surprised, therefore, that their patterns of speech lacked some of the specificity of the other deviant groups. More likely, the differences we found are characteristic of a group of depressives in relatively good remission. The alcoholics' potential for depression was revealed in their self-preoccupation, their concern with propriety and goodness, and their passive orientation toward the environment. The grosser manifestations of depression, reflected in paralinguistic disturbances and the extensive use of interpersonal manipulation, were absent. The clinical picture appears to us to be one of a population at risk and in remission. We can interpret their alcoholic consumption as a form of self-treatment for the control of dysphoric feelings.

Verbal Regression

In their attempts to understand the origins of psychopathology, psychoanalysts frequently compare the symptomatic acts of adult patients with the normal, phase-dependent behavior of children and adolescents. While analogy, according to Samuel Butler, may be the least misleading thing we have, its pitfalls in scientific speculation are obvious. We have certainly relied heavily upon this form of reasoning in trying to make sense of extremely complex data. What can we say about the possible similarities between the speech patterns of deviant adult patients and those of normal children and adolescents, specifically those we described in Chapter 3?

Although there are no perfect matches, we do have some interesting parallels. It comes as no surprise, for example, to learn that the impulsives resembled the midadolescents in certain respects. Both groups scored high in retractors, negatives, expressions of feeling, evaluators, and direct references. They differed primarily in the area of productivity: the adolescents had the highest score of any group we tested, whereas the impulsives were somewhat below the controls. The compulsives also showed a verbal pattern similar to that of the midadolescents, differing primarily in the greater use of the pronoun, *me*.

Our depressives may have undergone a true regression in their verbal behavior. Changes in productivity, rate, and pauses, associated with psychomotor retardation, brought their scores in these categories close to those of the kindergarten and first-grade children. We can observe other similarities between the two groups, such as their frequent use of expressions of feeling, *I*, and *me*, and their low nonpersonal references scores. Of all the groups we studied, the depressives and early schoolers had the greatest difficulty completing the experimental task.

Summary

We have demonstrated in this chapter that groups of individuals sharing deviant styles of thinking and behavior differed significantly from normal volunteers in a number of our speech categories. In many instances, the parallels between grammatical patterns and nonverbal symtomatology were striking and congruent with clinical descriptions in the literature. That significant findings emerged from comparisons of small groups suggests that our system of verbal behavior analysis is highly sensitive to nuances of style. Thematic content and verbal style appeared to be associated, indicating that interpretation of behavior from samples of speech does not require familiarity with lexical content.

Notes

1. No attempt was made to predict how depressives would compare with the controls in the various categories. Some of the patients in the depressed group were known to the experimenters who scored the verbal material. This was not true of the impulsives and delusionals for whom predictions were made. Familiarity on the part of the experimenters with the other three deviant groups (compulsives, binge-eaters, and alcoholics) similarly precluded predictions with these populations.

2. Since our deviant populations did not contain equal numbers of men and women, we must consider the possibility that significant differences between certain groups and the controls in a number of categories might be due to sex rather than pathology. To rule out this possibility, we performed *t* tests comparing each of the female deviant groups (binge-eaters and alcoholics) with the 23 female controls in those categories where sex differences had been demonstrated previously: *me*, retractors, explainers, and evaluators (see Chapter 3). Our data revealed no decrease in incidence of significance due to the exclusion of the male controls.

3. We have addressed the problem of patient status in a previous publication (Aronson & Weintraub, 1972). We demonstrated that the more-deviant groups did not have consistently more extreme scores than the less-deviant populations. It is

true that the control subjects did make the least or most use of certain mechanisms, but Table 4–2 shows that this was not the case in a number of categories. The binge-eating women, who were neither patients nor seriously disturbed, obtained scores, in a number of categories, that were as extreme as or more extreme than those of groups composed of patients requiring psychiatric hospitalization.

An absence of parallel structure for the group profiles, reflected in the failure of the same deviant populations consistently to score highest or lowest in the various categories, is persuasive evidence that the results cannot be accounted for entirely on the basis of patient status or undifferentiated pathology. In a number of our measures, deviant groups are sufficiently dissimilar to occupy both the highest and the lowest extreme positions when compared to nonpatient groups.

The data indicate that something beyond patient status or undifferentiated psychopathology is being measured. The directions of the differences among the various groups strongly suggest that verbal patterns are related to characteristic styles of thinking and behaving, which in turn reflect the operation of psychological coping mechanisms.

Chapter 5

Verbal Behavior Analysis of the Watergate Transcripts: A New Approach to Psychohistorical Research

Walter Weintraub and S. Michael Plaut

Thus far, we have shown that it is possible to study manifestations of psychological defense or coping mechanisms in speech by isolating categories that can be scored with adequate interjudge reliability. These categories appear to be related to clinically significant behavior, are used to different degrees by different individuals, and are determined by syntactic and paralinguistic, rather than semantic, criteria. We wish to emphasize this last point. Compared to content, form-related variables have a slower rate of change and are less subject to conscious manipulation by the speaker. They are, therefore, ideally suited to the investigation of personality traits, chronic symptomatology, and styles of thinking and behaving.

111

Verbal Behavior Analysis
Applied to Individuals

Since our system is both stable and reflective of general behavior, why not use it to study the speech patterns of individual subjects? Until now, we have been reluctant to do so because of the considerable variance in some categories and the infrequent use of certain mechanisms by many subjects. We believe that a 10-minute sample of speech does not provide an adequate data base upon which to synthesize the personality profile of a single person.

In his 1973 book, E. Steinberg, a British professor of English, demonstrated that a number of our categories could be applied usefully to the study of the personalities of the principal characters of James Joyce's *Ulysses*. Steinberg's contribution, however, went beyond character analysis. He showed that certain measures could be used to identify state-dependent reactions, such as changes in the quality of affective display. We shall return to this subject in Chapter 7, when we consider in detail the relationship between verbal style and emotional expression.

Despite serious procedural deficiencies and the fact that his work dealt with fictional characters communicating in a different medium, Steinberg's work encouraged us to accept the challenge of a University of Michigan psycholinguistic group to analyze "blind" several transcripts of recorded spontaneous speech samples prepared at Ann Arbor. Although the monologues averaged fewer than 1000 words per subject, we were able to construct personality profiles that, in the judgment of one of the Michigan investigators, indicated that our method had the ability "to accurately tap certain important personality dimensions" (Binder, 1975).

Publication
of the Watergate Transcripts

We were presented a golden opportunity to analyze the speech of well-known individuals when the transcripts of the Watergate tapes were published in 1974 (Committee on the Judiciary, 1974). To our knowledge, never before in history have spontaneous conversations involving important political leaders been electronically recorded and made available to the public. Since the actors in the Watergate drama can be assumed to have been under considerable stress during most of the published conversations, the transcripts should contain pertinent data relative to the adaptive patterns, as reflected in their styles of speaking, of the four individuals whose remarks made up the bulk of the recorded material.

Later in this chapter, we shall report the results of our verbal analysis of the Watergate transcripts. We shall try to determine, first of all, if one or more of the four principal conspirators, Richard Nixon, John Dean, H. R. Haldeman, and John Ehrlichman, revealed a style of speaking comparable to any of the groups of deviant individuals studied in Chapter 4. Secondly, we shall attempt to sketch personality profiles of the Watergate participants from the published material.

Problems of Method in Psychohistorical Research

The reader will note that we do not intend to follow the example of those psychobiographers who attempt detailed and elaborate psychodynamic formulations and psychogenetic reconstructions on the basis of selected incidents in the lives of historical figures. We believe that psychobiographies in the psychoanalytic tradition, even the best of them, suffer from the same procedural flaws as a psychoanalytic interpretation of a work of art. In the words of Paul Ricoeur (1970), such a study

> . . . cannot be compared to a therapeutic or didactic psychoanalysis, for the simple reason that it does not have the method of free association at its disposal, nor can it situate its interpretations in the field of the dual relation between doctor and patient. In this respect, the biographical documents available to art interpretation are of no more significance than the information furnished by a third party during a treatment. [p. 164]

In a genuine psychoanalysis, the patient's distortions of past events are irrelevant. Since the analyst is concerned primarily with psychic reality, the validity of his interpretations can be tested by the analysand's associative responses. Changes in levels of resistance, the discovery of fresh recollections, and the recognition of new, meaningful connections are all indications that a useful psychoanalytic intervention has been made. The fact that such validation is impossible in psychobiography has not prevented its practitioners from resorting to the use of apocryphal material in their attempts to understand the motives of historical subjects.

An excellent example of the careless handling of historical data is to be found in Erikson's use of the so-called "fit in the choir," which supposedly possessed Martin Luther as a young man (Lifton, 1972). After admitting that the historical evidence for the actual occurrence of the incident is not strong, Erikson nevertheless places heavy emphasis upon the "event" to help reconstruct a psychoanalytic understanding of Luther (Erikson, 1958, pp. 23–38). The fact that Luther himself apparently never mentioned the incident and that many of his biographers deny the story are dismissed by Erikson since, in his view, "the making of legend is as much part of the scholarly rewriting of history as it is part of the original facts used in the work of scholars." We are, according to Erikson, permitted to use not only the manifest content of well-established events but even the gossip and fantasies of contemporaries in arriving at a psychoanalytic understanding of an historical figure, "provided only that a reported episode does not contradict other well-established facts; persists in having a ring of truth; and yields a meaning consistent with psychological theory."

Some of the problems inherent in psychohistorical research have been reviewed by Lifton (1972). The procedural problems remain, whether one chooses to approach history as Freud did, as little more than "psychological recurrence"; or as Erikson has, as "the intersection of individual and collective histories"; or as Lifton and his colleagues have, as "shared psychohistorical themes as observed in men and women exposed to particular kinds of experiences." The historical figure, in Lifton's words, "tends to be inaccessible, at least to direct interview, or if accessible not yet great. One usually must approach him through records or . . . through interviews with surviving friends and fellows . . . problems of reconstruction become inevitable."

Recognizing versus Understanding the Historical Figure

One of the consequences of weaving psychological themes from limited historical evidence is that as the analysis moves forward, the identity of the subject begins to fade. "Understanding" often is achieved at the price of recognition. Since the psychobiographer usually is more interested in developing a particular psychological or historical theory than he is in the thinking and behavior of his chosen subject, universal themes commonly are stressed to the virtual exclusion of individual variations. It is most doubtful if any of the historical figures whose lives and minds have been dissected by psychoanalytic biographers could be recognized by historians solely on the basis of dynamic and genetic formulations.

When applied to biographical studies, the psychoanalytic method inevitably obscures the greatness of the subject. Readers of psychobiographies are often at a loss to account for the extraordinary accomplishments of historical figures subjected to analytic scrutiny. In his search for meaning, the psychohistorian deals with the derivatives of a finite number of universal drives and phase-specific conflicts. The approach is essentially reductionistic and usually disappointing in its failure to explain outstanding achievement, let alone genius.

We must reconstruct the personalities of historical figures from the infinite variety of ego and superego structures that "serve simultaneously internal drive restriction and external adaptation" (Freud, 1965, p. 177). Attempts to clarify the unconscious conflicts of public figures can never rise above the level of wild analysis, no matter how intuitive the biographer may be. The surface manifestations of ego and superego functions, on the other hand, are subject to observation and objective recording in a variety of settings. Much greater attention must be paid to the conflict-free areas of ego functioning if we wish to enlarge our understanding of that which distinguishes the makers of history from the rest of humanity.

Of course, procedural limitations do not account for all the problems of the psychobiographer. According to Meyer (1972), "serious difficulties in the application of psychoanalysis to biography result from emotional factors residing in the biographer and notably in his relationships to his subject." This source of bias is impossible to eliminate, in Meyer's opinion, since the same "emotional factors" that warp the biographer's judgment provide him with the necessary incentive to undertake the study in the first place.

Free Speech and Writing
Ignored by Psychohistorians

If psychobiographers have been less than fastidious in their handling of anecdotal information, their failure to make adequate use of certain historical data is even more noteworthy. Although a great deal of free speech and writing has been available to psychoanalytic biographers in the form of letters, diaries, and recorded interviews, few, if any, have attempted psycholinguistic analyses of their subjects' verbal productions. When such materials have been used, attention usually has been paid only to thematic content; the formal characteristics of the historical figure's communications, so revealing of personality, generally have been ignored.

A New Approach to
Psychohistorical Research

In this chapter, a new and, we hope, more systematic approach to psychohistory will be tried. We shall resist the temptation to make intrusive excursions into the inner world of historical figures on the basis of anecdotal information. In the case of the Watergate conspirators, such an attempt would be an unwarranted and unethical invasion of the privacy of living individuals. The study we shall describe was designed to shed light on certain questions of legitimate public interest. We have relied entirely upon data available to everyone; our method of analysis can be learned from published reports and requires no special intuitive powers. Although each reader can decide individually whether and how an understanding of the participants' motivations can be enlarged from the results of our project, we are more interested in the recognition of ego and superego functions than the understanding of universal desires. Can the identity, personalities, and behavior of the four Watergate participants, well known to the public from news reports and television interviews, be recognized from their speech patterns? If the answer proves to be yes, we will have taken a modest step in establishing psychohistory on a firmer, empirical footing. Psychobiographers then will be in a position to apply a method like ours to historical figures whose personalities and behavior are less well known than those of the Watergate conspirators.

One of the factors that led to our decision to analyze the Watergate transcripts is the large quantity of raw data available for the study. We have at our disposal approximately 20 times more transcribed material than was provided for us by the University of Michigan group for their subjects. Of the 14 categories, only 10 can be used with transcribed speech samples. Productivity, rate, and silences cannot be scored without access to the tapes themselves. The fourth category, which measures direct references to the experimenter or experimental procedure, can be determined only if the verbal samples are collected in the laboratory, according to the method described in Chapter 2.

Verbal Analysis of the Watergate Transcripts

For each of the four participants, Nixon, Haldeman, Ehrlichman, and Dean, we selected 20 samples of 1000 words each from the Watergate transcripts. (Because of his peculiarly laconic style, only 16 samples could be assembled for Haldeman.) The samples were made up from randomly chosen entries exceeding 30 words. We decided to use only entries having at least 30 words, in order to minimize the effect of dialogue. As we shall see in Chapter 7, there are certain structural differences between monologues and dialogues. In general, the longer the excerpt, the more it resembles a monologue in its formal linguistic characteristics.

A group of 23 male, armed-forces volunteers, described in Chapter 2, were used as a control group. The samples were scored for the following 10 categories:

1. Nonpersonal references.
2. I.
3. We.
4. Me.
5. Negatives.
6. Qualifiers.
7. Retractors.
8. Explainers.
9. Expressions of feeling.
10. Evaluators.

A percentile ranking was done of the normal male controls, as well as of the groups of depressives, impulsives, delusionals and compulsives described in Chapter 4, for each of the ten categories, in order to determine the relative position of each Watergate participant in those samples. It was assumed that if the participant fell above or below 90 percent of the sample scores, he could be considered deviant for that category with respect to the group in question.

In addition, the observations for each of the four subjects were ranked, and semi-interquartile ranges (SIQR) were determined by computing half the difference between scores representing the 25th and 75th percentiles. The possibility of differences among the four subjects for each category was determined by Kruskal-Wallis one-way analysis of variance (Siegel, 1956). Where significant results were obtained, pairs of subjects were compared by Mann-Whitney U-tests (Siegel, 1956).

The data show that, compared to the male controls, Nixon used more evaluators and negatives, while Haldeman used more negatives and fewer expressions of feeling. Neither Dean nor Ehrlichman deviated from the controls in any of the 10 categories. When we compared the scores of the 4 Watergate participants with those of the groups of depressives, impulsives, delusionals, and compulsives, we found that, with the exception of Nixon, all differed in at least 2 categories from the 4 deviant populations. Nixon could not be distinguished from the depressives in any of the 10 categories; he differed from the impulsives only in his use of I. (Medians for the 10 speech categories are shown in Figures 5–1 and 5–2.) Occurrence of significant differences between pairs of subjects are shown in Table 5–1, and the overall incidence of differences between individuals is illustrated in Figure 5–3.

Our results give no support to allegations that Nixon or his close collaborators were suffering from paranoid or compulsive disorders. The data are, however, consistent with suggestions that the former President may have been clinically depressed during the time the conversations were recorded. Also noteworthy are indications of an impulsive side to Nixon's character; an extraordinary inability or disinclination on the part of Haldeman to express feelings; and a high frequency of occurrence of negatives in the speech of both Nixon and Haldeman.

Personality Profiles of Watergate Participants

We now shall attempt to sketch personality profiles of Nixon and his three White House aides. These profiles will be constructed from the list of significant differences among the four subjects in the various categories. Again, it is important to note that what we will be seeking are areas of correspondence between speech and behavior, on the one hand, and psychological coping mechanisms, on the other. We shall make few speculations about the subjects' motivations, contrary to what has been the fashion of psychoanalytic biographers.

Nixon

Compared to the other participants, Nixon's scores are high in the following categories: *I, me, we,* expressions of feeling, negatives, retractors, and evaluators; his use of nonpersonal references is low. Assumptions about the psychological defense mechanisms mirrored by these verbal categories, discussed in Chapter 2, as well as the scores of the psychiatrically deviant groups, presented in Chapter 4, allow us to suggest the following about the former President.

The low nonpersonal references score, together with the rather frequent use of *I* and *me*, indicate a tendency on Nixon's part to speak in a concrete, personal manner. During the recorded conversations, he was concerned primarily with himself and people and events known to him, rather than with abstract ideas. The expressions of feeling score tells us that, among the four participants, Nixon was the least inhibited in expressing affect. A high negatives score suggests not only a generally resistant attitude but also a need to deny unpleasant aspects of reality. Nixon's frequent use of retractors indicates a strong tendency to reconsider, to reverse himself after decisions are made. This lends a certain quality of vacillation or impulsivity to his verbal style. His high evaluators score can be translated into a concern for the moral and ethical consequences of his actions or, at the very least, for how his behavior might appear to others.

The fact that the former President is neither high nor low in the

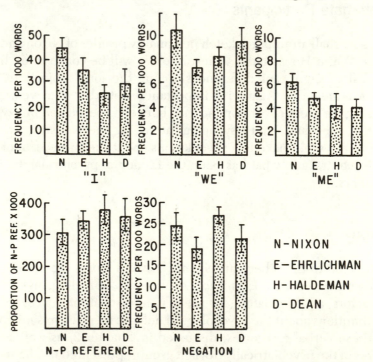

Figure 5–1. Use of Verbal Categories by Four Watergate Participants, Based upon 16 to 20 Speech Samples per Subject.

categories of qualifiers and explainers indicates that he had no serious problems making decisions and that he really did not try to explain matters to any great extent, despite his often-stated desire to make things perfectly clear. A close reading of the Watergate transcripts shows that Nixon was more apt to make dogmatic, categorical remarks than carefully reasoned ones.

In summary, Nixon's speech is rather concrete and is centered around himself and people and events familiar to him. More than his former aides, he is able to express feelings. He can make decisions but tends to vacillate and is capable of impulsively reversing himself. He may deny unpleasant aspects of reality and can be moralistic and dogmatic; he has a tendency to voice opinions rather than reasoned judgments. In terms of resemblance to deviant psychiatric populations, Nixon's speech can be compared to that of the groups of depressive and impulsive patients.

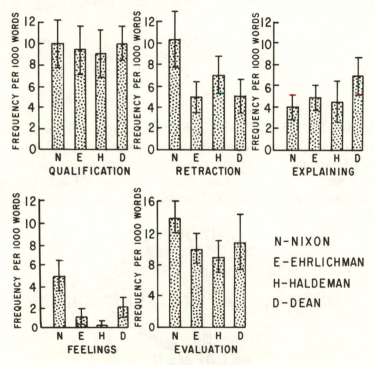

Figure 5–2. Use of Verbal Categories by Four Watergate Participants, Based upon 16 to 20 Speech Samples per Subject.

If Nixon was indeed depressed during the period of time the conversations were recorded, it is possible that his scores in categories like *I* and nonpersonal references could change with an alteration of mood. In a previously published report, we showed that as patients recovered from episodes of depression, their productivity and silence scores significantly changed (Aronson & Weintraub, 1967b). The whole problem of state- versus trait-dependent paralinguistic and syntactic variables is a complex one; it will be considered at length in Chapter 7.

The following excerpts from the Watergate transcripts (Committee on the Judiciary, 1974) convey something of the flavor of Nixon's vacillation, particularly when under pressure:

> The report was not frankly accurate. Well it was accurate but it was not full. And he tells me the reason it wasn't full, was that he didn't know. Whether that is true or not, I don't know. Although it wasn't I'm told. But I'm satisfied with it. [p. 860]

> That isn't the problem. The problem is not the fact that we can't run the shop. We can run the shop, maybe not as well, but we can run it. But on the other hand. . . . [p. 361]

Dean

Compared to Nixon, Dean demonstrates a somewhat more impersonal style. There is a greater use of nonpersonal references and fewer *I*'s and *me*'s. Dean's use of expressions of feeling, although not high compared to the normal controls, is second only to Nixon's among the four participants. His negatives score is not particularly

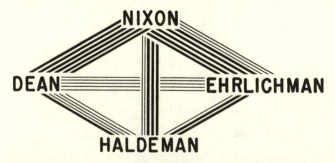

Figure 5–3. Incidence of Significant Differences between Pairs of Subjects for the 10 Verbal Categories (−*p*< .05, −*p* < .01).

high, compared to that of the other three, suggesting a generally positive approach to others as well as an ability to consider and judge both favorable and disagreeable sides of reality. A moderate qualifiers score reflects an unimpaired ability to make decisions and commitments. In the retractors category, Dean's score is significantly below that of Nixon's and Haldeman's; he does not reverse decisions once they are made. There is no evidence of impulsivity or brashness in his speech.

Dean used more explainers than any of the other Watergate participants. This tendency to reason and to justify gives his speech a certain intellectual flavor. The relatively high explainers score— above the mean of the normal controls, although not significantly so—may indicate a need to rationalize thoughts and behavior to himself and others. Dean also has a rather high evaluators score. Only Nixon shows a greater sensitivity toward questions of right and wrong, propriety and appropriateness.

In summary, Dean's speech reflects more of a reasoning, "intellectual" style than that of the other conspirators. He has a generally positive approach to people and events, can make decisions, is able to express feelings and evidences no signs of vacillation or impulsivity. Dean definitely is concerned about questions of morality and propriety. Compared to Nixon, he is less concrete and more imper-

Table 5–1. Statistical Comparison of Subjects

Variable	H (df = 3)	Significant Differences‡
Negatives	16.58†	H > D; E < N, H
Qualifiers	2.53	—
Retractors	22.90†	H < D; N > E, D
Explainers	11.02*	D > N, E
Feelings	42.19†	N > E, H, D; H < E, D
Evaluators	18.05†	N > E, H; D > E, H
N-P References	17.34†	N < E, H, D
I	38.10†	N > H, E, D; E > H, D; D > H
We	8.38*	N > E; D > E
Me	11.55†	N > H, E, D; E > D

*p < 0.05
†P < 0.01
‡N = Nixon; E = Ehrlichman; H = Haldeman; D = Dean

sonal in his communicative style. Dean's scores suggest no significant degree of psychopathology.

Typical of Dean's cautious, impersonal, explanatory style of
communication are the following excerpts (Committee on the
Judiciary, 1974):

> The reason that I thought we ought to talk this morning is because in
> our conversations, I have the impression that you don't know every-
> thing I know. [p. 172]

> Well, as I say, I haven't probed Sullivan to the depths on this thing
> because I want to treat him at arm's length until he is safe, because he
> has a world of information that may be available. [p. 95]

> Because, I understand that after the fact that there was a plan to bug
> Larry O'Brien's suite down in Florida. So Liddy told me that this is
> what had happened and this is why it had happened. [p. 181]

Haldeman

Of the 4 Watergate conspirators, Haldeman has the highest nonpersonal references and the lowest *I* and expressions of feeling scores.
These findings go a long way to account for the impersonal, mechanical quality of his speech. Haldeman's infrequent use of feeling
words is quite remarkable. In this category, he not only differs
significantly from the other Watergate subjects, but his score is less
than 90 percent of the sample scores of the normal controls and of all
4 psychiatrically deviant populations. Haldeman also has a higher
negatives score than his 3 colleagues, an interesting finding in view
of his reputation as the "Abominable No-man." The high negatives
score conceivably may indicate a tendency to place a wall between
himself and others and to deny entrance to stimuli that challenge
cherished beliefs and attitudes.

Haldeman's qualifiers score is neither high nor low, suggesting
no major difficulties in making decisions and commitments. His
retractors score is rather elevated, second only to that of Nixon's.
This finding reflects a capacity to reconsider, possibly a streak of
impulsivity.

With respect to explainers, Haldeman's score is neither high
nor low. Like Nixon, he was more apt to make categorical state-

ments than to offer reasons for thoughts and actions. Haldeman's evaluators score is also moderate. Despite the extremely sensitive nature of the material discussed in the Watergate transcripts, his speech samples reveal no great preoccupation with questions of right and wrong.

To summarize, Haldeman emerges as rather impersonal and cold. Compared to his White House colleagues, he is a laconic "no" man who establishes firm barriers and perhaps denies disagreeable aspects of reality. Haldeman can make decisions without hesitation but there apparently is a tendency to reconsider, a touch of impulsivity. Explaining or justification is not a Haldeman trait; he states his point of view dogmatically, often in the language of the advertising man or in the form of "scenarios," considering the possible consequences of hypothetical actions without either expressing feelings about or judging the propriety of the imagined behavior.

Like Nixon's, Haldeman's scores deviate from those of the normal controls in 3 of the 10 categories. His scores also differ from each of the 4 psychiatrically deviant populations in at least 2 categories. If, on the basis of his differences from the normal controls, Haldeman deserves to be placed in a deviant psychological group, it is clearly not one that we have studied.

Haldeman's frequent use of negatives and retractors, as well as his impersonal, mechanical creation of "scenarios," are well illustrated in the following quotations from the transcripts (Committee on the Judiciary, 1974):

> There isn't a feeling on his part of a desire to get people, but a desire to take care of himself. And that he might be willing to do what he had to do to take care of himself, but he would probably do it on a gradual basis. [p. 327]

> Let me suggest a different process, which is that you don't suspend John Dean, but that you instruct John Dean that he is not to come to work anymore. He is in effect suspended but not publicly suspended. [p. 1001]

> It is a problem for us, there is no question about it, but there is no way he can prove it. [p. 536]

Ehrlichman

Compared to the other 3 subjects, Ehrlichman scores rather low in negatives and expressions of feeling; he is neither high nor low in any of the other 8 categories. In a sense, his speech pattern is the least distinctive of the 4 participants. Although we made no attempt to measure the verbal productivity of the various conspirators during the recorded conversations, Ehrlichman appears to deserve his reputation as one of Nixon's more loquacious aides. Of 6 Watergate entries exceeding 300 words, 5 entries were spoken by Ehrlichman. On the other hand, so many of Haldeman's remarks were under 30 words that it was possible to gather only 16 samples of 1000 words for him.

Next to Nixon, Ehrlichman is the least impersonal of the four subjects, as measured by his nonpersonal references and *I* scores. Because of the relative scarcity of feeling words, there is, nevertheless, a certain mechanical quality to his speech. Ehrlichman can make decisions, and, once taken, they are not retracted. There is no evidence of the kind of vacillation present in Nixon's, and to a lesser extent in Haldeman's samples. Ehrlichman resembles Haldeman in his frequent use of "scenarios," discussing at great length the likely consequences of imagined actions. There is little in the way of feelings expressed about these actions or of their propriety. Ehrlichman shares with Nixon and Haldeman (but not Dean!) a tendency toward dogmatic discourse. He makes few attempts to explain or justify thoughts or behavior. Of the four participants, he is the least negative, perhaps the one best able to consider all facets of reality.

In summary, Ehrlichman's verbal style seems voluble and mechanical. His speech profile reflects decisiveness and an ability to adhere to decisions. Compared to his White House colleagues, he shows more openness to a variety of points of view, yet his speech is dogmatic rather than explanatory and shows little concern about the propriety of actions being discussed. Like Dean, Ehrlichman's scores do not differ from those of the normal controls in any of the 10 verbal categories. With respect to the 4 psychiatrically deviant populations, Ehrlichman differs from each of them in at least 2 categories. His style of speaking, as measured by our system, reveals no significant psychopathology.

Although Ehrlichman's speaking style is the least deviant of the

Watergate conspirators, his frequent use of "scenarios" lends a certain pragmatic flavor to his communications. These scenarios generally are spoken in the present tense, imparting a sense of drama and immediacy to his comments, as the following excerpts (Committee on the Judiciary, 1974) show:

> O.K. He reviews it. He gets the complete file with the pros and cons. He goes through it and he draws on seven years experience and he comes over to you and he says, "I've got to call this shot and I wonder if you have anything to add." [p. 1053]

> You've got Dean coming in to you saying, "I've talked to the U.S. Attorney and I've told him a lot of things that I did wrong." So you put him on leave. He isn't charged with anything yet, but he's said them to you. [p. 992]

> And then, let them come back and say, "No, that isn't what we mean. We mean it can be taped." And then we'll come back and say, "Well, that isn't satisfactory." By that time, they're in a recess. [p. 944]

Deriving Personality Profiles from Verbal Data

How can we be sure that our profiles have been derived from the verbal data and not from knowledge of the Watergate subjects obtained in other ways? Would we have constructed similar profiles if the identities of the participants had been unknown to us?

In order to rule out the possibility that the 4 personality profiles could not be derived directly from the verbal data, we deleted from them all references that might identify the participants or the relationship of the study to the Watergate affair. The abbreviated profiles, a written description of the 10 categories, and the scores of the participants were presented to a group of 10 freshman medical students enrolled in a psychiatric interviewing course. The students were asked to match each of the profiles with the appropriate set of scores. Nothing was said to them about Watergate; they simply were informed that the profiles and scores belonged to 4 experimental subjects. (The full texts of the abbreviated profiles can be found in Appendix B.)

Correct matches were made by the students in all 10 cases for Nixon ($\chi^2 = 30.0$, $df = 1$, $p < .001$); in 8 cases for Dean and Haldeman ($\chi^2 = 16.5$, $df = 1$, $p < .001$), and in 9 cases for Ehrlichman ($\chi^2 = 22.5$, $df = 1$, $p < .001$). These results indicate that the personality profiles of the Watergate subjects could be identified from their scores. We need not assume that conscious or unconscious use of other sources of information about the participants was made by us in constructing the profiles.

Influence of Context on Watergate Conversations

Are we justified in drawing conclusions from the Watergate transcripts based partly upon comparisons with groups of individuals who provided speech samples under laboratory conditions? The transcripts are records of conversations among two or more individuals, whereas the material with which we have compared them consists of samples of free speech collected in the presence of a silent experimenter. The literature contains many assertions to the effect that verbal behavior is affected both in content and form by a number of environmental factors. We have every reason to believe, nevertheless, that categories having a slow rate of change reflect characteristic verbal behavior, particularly when applied to conversations recorded over a period of months.

It is important for us to consider, however, some of the ways in which differences in data collection might have biased our results in a certain direction. It has been claimed, on the basis of anecdotal information, that "we all have many languages, perhaps as many as the social situations in which we participate" (Jaffe, 1960a). In earlier chapters, we considered some of the variables that have been said to influence styles of communication. They include the number of individuals involved in the communications network, the social distance of the persons involved, their truthfulness, and the social status of the participants.

Compared to the Watergate transcripts, the data we collected in the laboratory were gathered under conditions of greater social distance; the degree of candor was probably of quite a different order; and the number of participating individuals, as well as their hierarchal relationships, differed. We might wonder about the possible effect on the verbal styles of the Watergate participants of the various roles they played in the administration. Figure 5–3 shows that Nixon's verbal behavior stands out as most different from that of the others. Is this finding a reflection of differences in personality and state of mind at the time, or can part or all of it be attributed to the fact that he was the most powerful of the four? It can be argued that the former chief executive's higher expressions of feeling and retractors scores are due to the fact that as president, he could permit himself a certain flexibility denied to subordinates. A leader can blow off steam or play with ideas more easily than less powerful assistants. The fact that Haldeman and Ehrlichman resemble each other in their speaking styles may be more a function of the similarity of their roles in the Nixon administration than of their personalities. Dean's precise, explanatory manner of speaking also can be seen as reflecting his position, both as legal advisor to the former President and as the key conspirator who had the most to explain away among the four participants.

To what extent were the Watergate subjects influenced in their verbal behavior by the fact that they were engaged in conversations rather than spontaneous monologues? Does the finding that all four participants score rather high in the negatives category reflect a common personality characteristic, or can we assume that spirited conversation may have elicited oppositional tendencies?

These speculations lead us to confess that we simply do not know how verbal style, as we measure it, is affected by the various factors we have just considered. Most studies dealing with role and communication have used paralinguistic, rather than syntactic, variables. Claims that verbal style shifts with changing social context rely almost entirely upon clinical observations.

Comparison of Speech and Behavior of Watergate Participants

Many journalists, historians, and biographers have discussed the personalities and behavior of the Watergate subjects (Rather & Gates, 1974; Higgins, 1974). All four conspirators have been on public display while performing their official duties, testifying before Congressional committees and in court, and responding to reporters' questions on television. Without going into such controversial questions as the integrity or competence of our subjects, we wish to take some of the character traits attributed to them by observers and see how they may be (or may not be!) reflected in the speech patterns we have described. We believe that the following descriptions of the Watergate conspirators are reasonably objective and relatively free of pejorative connotations.

Nixon

The former President is a highly intelligent, analytical, and ambitious man. In a variety of ways, he is competitive, even combative. An admirer of well-bred, graceful people, Nixon can be socially awkward and physically clumsy. In the presence of individuals he greatly respects, his behavior appears deferential, almost obsequious. Most observers agree that he is an extraordinarily vulnerable man in his personal relationships; he is very sensitive to slights and is appreciative of praise and loyalty. Nixon appears to be fearful of unstructured situations. He is methodical and well prepared for his assignments; he is said to be an avid reader and a good listener.

The former President is considered to be a private, even a solitary man. He prefers the company of reserved, unemotional, and predictable individuals, although for brief periods of time he enjoys and can profit intellectually from the stimulation of flamboyant personalities. Generally able to pursue logical, carefully conceived plans, Nixon, under pressure, can behave in vacillating, contradictory, and even irrational ways. This tends to occur when he feels threatened by rivals or enemies.

To all except family and a few close associates, Nixon appears distant and aloof. Despite a combative temperament, he dislikes personal confrontations. It is difficult for him to be insulting or even severe with anyone in personal, one-to-one encounters. Although he does not cultivate kindliness as part of his public image, Nixon has been known to perform many quiet acts of generosity.

Up to a point, it is easy to correlate Nixon's personality traits, as just described, with his pattern of verbal behavior. We can interpret his tendency to blurt out and retract, so noticeable in the transcripts, as an expression of his disorganization and vacillation under stress. Critics of the former President may see in his high retractors score evidence of deception, of talking out of both sides of his mouth at the same time (some of this can be seen in the verbatim examples quoted in the previous section). Nixon's concrete, personal style also has been on public display during moments of crisis. When at his combative best, as in the "Checkers" speech, he has been able to use this approach with great rhetorical effect. When intimidated or defeated, as in the 1960 presidential campaign, the California gubernatorial race, and after his resignation from the presidency, Nixon's speaking style has had a rambling, almost incoherent quality. His need for structure and order, as well as his preference for low-key associates, may stem from a realization that he is subject to disorganization under stress.

We have interpreted Nixon's frequent use of negatives, in part, as evidence of his not being able to look at all aspects of reality. Under pressure, particularly when besieged by enemies, Nixon has at times shown very poor judgment in political matters. We can attribute his downfall to a tendency to overestimate the hostility and dangerousness of his opponents and to underestimate the seriousness of the Watergate affair.

How are we to explain Nixon's high evaluators score? Although cynics might contend that his conscience has tolerated gross ethical lapses during his political career, the former President has been and continues to be preoccupied with his performance and image. His speeches and press conferences have been full of evaluators. He wanted his administration to have "good marks" on historians' report cards; his defense of his Vietnam policy rested on his desire to do the "right thing." Perhaps even more importantly, Nixon's fear of ridicule has made him very conscious of his public appearance. To be always correct, proper, and appropriate has been such an obsession with him that it was possible for a California public relations man to become the second most powerful official in his administration.

Haldeman

Of the various presidential aides, Haldeman was probably most loyal to Nixon and least ambitious for himself. He believed both in Nixon, the man, and in the conservative, anti-Communist program the former President espoused. To help Nixon achieve his goals,

Haldeman brought considerable organizational talent. There is general agreement that he is efficient, crisp, and almost military in his self-control and intolerance of sloppiness. He carried out Nixon's orders without question and expected the same automatic obedience from his subordinates.

Haldeman has been described as secretive, shy, and arrogant, with a strong sense of image. With Nixon he was deferential to the point of obsequiousness. He was rarely seen to show emotion in public, and his behavior when alone with Nixon and other associates was low-key. When caught in acts of political wrong-doing, Haldeman showed no remorse, apparently believing that a higher purpose was being served. Spurning personal publicity, he preferred a quiet life at home to the Washington cocktail-party circuit. Haldeman protected Nixon's privacy by controlling access to the Oval Office. He apparently derived satisfaction and pleasure from his reputation as Nixon's "S.O.B." and the President's "No-man."

Although efficient and competent in matters of organization, Haldeman's judgment in political and legal matters was flawed. He showed a great lack of understanding of the seriousness of the Watergate affair until near the very end, minimizing and denying the implications of John Dean's messages. He proved himself extremely loyal to Nixon, apparently willing to sacrifice his career and reputation to serve the former President. Only when Nixon proved unworthy of his loyalty did Haldeman feel free to pursue an independent course of action.

Which of Haldeman's personality traits can be seen in his pattern of verbal behavior? The military, stoic, impersonal qualities come across quite clearly in the high nonpersonal references and low *I* scores. We can interpret the latter finding as a concrete indication of Haldeman's subjugation of his own ego and personality to that of Nixon's. His mechanical, brusque manner is mirrored by a remarkably low expressions of feeling score. Considering the nature of the material under discussion, this finding is extremely interesting.

It is almost amusing to discover that Nixon's "Abominable No-man" scores the highest among the four subjects in the negatives category. In our opinion, this use of negatives reflects more than Haldeman's "gatekeeping" function. The former President's chief aide was known to be narrowly loyal to Nixon and his conservative ideology. His political and legal errors can be attributed, to a considerable extent, to an inability or unwillingness to evaluate unpleasant data. Haldeman, like Nixon, was unable to appreciate the seriousness of the Watergate affair until it was too late. He, like the former President, was isolated from people and information that could have provided useful perspective.

Haldeman's evaluators scores do not reveal a troubled conscience or a preoccupation with what is good and moral. This fits well with his reputation as a ruthless fanatic who would do anything for Nixon and his programs, without compunction or remorse. In carrying out his leader's wishes, Haldeman suppressed not only his ego but, to an even greater extent, merged his superego with that of the former President.

We have referred already to Haldeman's unimpaired ability to make decisions and his dogmatic rather than explanatory style of discourse. The one surprise in his speech pattern is a rather high retractors score. This generally reflects a certain impulsive quality, and Haldeman, to our knowledge, has not been described in this way. It is possible that in presenting his "scenarios," he allowed his mind to consider opposing courses of action, a practice that would result in a high retractors score. Perhaps we have discovered an aspect of his personality heretofore hidden from the public.

Ehrlichman

John Ehrlichman's personality, as reflected in his public behavior, can be described as follows: he generally was considered to be a hardworking, tireless, efficient administrator with a passion for detail. Forceful and decisive, he approached tasks in a thoughtful manner and could see different sides of a question. Although preferring to avoid the limelight, he was relaxed in public situations; he had a good sense of humor; and he impressed observers as an open, enthusiastic, and gregarious individual. Ehrlichman was ideologically more flexible than Haldeman; his loyalties as a presidential assistant were primarily to Nixon. Under pressure or in competitive situations, Ehrlichman could become arrogant and sarcastic; he was not above intimidating weaker opponents or subordinates; yet, he was known as a person who could, on occasion, make thoughtful gestures to low-level White House staff.

In comparing Ehrlichman's publicly visible personality traits with his speech mannerisms, we should begin by noting that there is little that is markedly deviant in the one or the other. His crisp, efficient, somewhat brusque way of conducting business may be reflected in a low expressions of feeling score. Ehrlichman's moderate qualifiers and retractors scores mirror his ability to decide without vacillation or regret. His nonpersonal references and *I* scores suggest a good balance between concrete and abstract concerns. No strong need to rationalize thoughts and behavior is present, and evidence of a troubled conscience, as reflected in a high evaluators score, is not obvious. It appears that Ehrlichman, like Haldeman, may have looked to Nixon for moral guidance. Ehrlichman's openness to people and ideas is reflected by a rather low negatives score. Although sometimes bracketed with Haldeman as a guardian of the "Berlin Wall," he does not emerge, in our analysis, as quite so forbidding and aloof. Ehrlichman's style does resemble that of Haldeman in ways not measured by our instrument. Both use the mechanical lingo of the West-Coast advertising executive, a practice apparently foreign to the temperaments of Nixon and Dean.

Dean

John Dean, like most of Nixon's aides, has been described as competent, industrious, and efficient. Unlike Haldeman, Ehrlichman, and certain others on the White House staff, his loyalty to the former President was that of an employee rather than that of a political follower. Observers have judged Dean to be temperamentally incapable of the kind of fanatical devotion demonstrated by Haldeman and Ehrlichman. He was, in the final analysis, loyal to himself and his career. In pursuing his own ends and those of his employer, Dean showed great technical skill and resourcefulness. He appeared outwardly unperturbed and extremely practical. What was most striking about Dean was his shrewd assessment of events and personalities. He was the supreme realist, not taken in by rhetoric or blinded by desire. He was always cautious and never impulsive. A careerist through and through, there was never a hint that he was motivated by any ideals higher than self-advancement and, at the end, self-preservation.

How can we relate Dean's speech pattern to this summary of his public behavior? His cautious, carefully reasoned approach to problems is reflected in a rather high explainers score. His moderately high use of nonpersonal references and rather low *I* score mirror a certain detachment and objectivity necessary for cool, accurate judgment. Most interesting, perhaps, is Dean's infrequent use of negatives, a finding that corresponds well with his reputation as a realist. He was open to all suggestions and turned his back on no workable plan.

Dean's moderate qualifiers and retractors scores indicate that, cautious as he was, he had no problems making decisions and sticking to them. What do we make, however, of the relatively high evaluators score? How can we attribute a concern for what is right and proper to a man who has been pictured as a cold-blooded, self-serving mercenary? It seems to us that, unlike Haldeman and Ehrlichman, Dean was acutely aware that illegal acts were being committed. He saw his job as conspiring to keep the incriminating details secret. He did not pretend to himself or to his White House superiors that what had happened was justified or legal. He may not have been terribly preoccupied with the morality of the Watergate break-in and cover-up, but he did recognize from the beginning the illegal nature of the acts. He knew right from wrong; not all of his colleagues shared this appreciation.

Limitations of Verbal Behavior Analysis for Use in Psychohistorical Research

It is clear from our attempts to relate personality to verbal behavior that much that is known about the Watergate participants is not reflected in their patterns of speaking, at least as measured by our categories. Certain, but by no means all, aspects of their characters are tapped by our system. Much that is important to the psychobiographer apparently cannot be gleaned from the data. Undoubtedly, new categories are necessary to obtain a broader view; perhaps the verbal approach itself has limitations.

Readers familiar with psychoanalytic studies of historical figures may miss the richness of intimate detail and the speculative
leaps that are lacking here. Meyer (1972) captured the euphoric,
unfettered feeling of the psychoanalytic historian when he wrote, in
mock enthusiasm, "How fortunate are we psychoanalytic biographers! We have an answer for nearly everything." Our approach
has been to try to broaden the base of reliable historical data, rather
than to look for psychological and historical explanations. Character
analysis of historical figures cannot be more precise than the information available to the biographer.

Summary

In this chapter, we have reported the results of the application of our
system of verbal behavior analysis to the Watergate transcripts.
Comparisons of samples of transcribed speech with a normal control
group and populations of delusional, impulsive, depressive, and
compulsive patients indicate no evidence of deviant verbal behavior
in the cases of Dean and Ehrlichman. Both Nixon and Haldeman
differ from the control subjects in 3 of 10 categories. The former
President cannot be distinguished from the depressives in any of the
verbal categories and deviates from the impulsives in only one.
Haldeman's style appears to be deviant but unlike any of the patient
groups.

We sketched personality profiles of the four conspirators by
comparing samples of their speech with each other and with the four
patient groups. It was possible to demonstrate in the speaking styles
of the Watergate participants reflections of personality traits
observed in their public behavior.

Chapter 6
A Comparison of Spoken and Written Language

Despite its obvious convenience as a source of verbal data, clinical investigators have shown little interest in the study of free writing. As recently as 1960, Gottschalk & Gleser complained of a "paucity of published investigations on microscopic analysis of word choice in written communication of a personal nature." We believe that clinicians have neglected written messages because speech is the medium through which diagnostic interviewing and psychotherapy are conducted.

Although psychotherapists occasionally have published analyses of written documents—Freud's analysis of Schreber's memoirs is a classic example—the systematic, clinical scrutiny of free writing has been limited, for the most part, to suicide notes. Due to unavoidable procedural flaws, these latter studies have been of only limited interest (Gottschalk & Gleser, 1960; Osgood & Walker, 1959; Schneidman, 1973; Tuckman, Kleiner, & Lavell, 1959).

In this chapter, we shall apply our method of verbal behavior analysis to the study of free writing. Since we do not use categories based upon phonological variables, our system should be applicable to nonspoken communication.

Analyzing written messages has the great practical advantage of eliminating the time-consuming task of transcribing spoken language into written symbols. More importantly, a great deal of clinical and historical material is available to us in written form. Diaries, letters, memoirs, memoranda, and the like are rich sources of clinical data; we lack only the techniques to analyze and interpret them.

Although a number of investigators have applied our system to spoken language, only one has used the method to study written material. In 1973, Steinberg reported using certain of our categories to analyze the characters of James Joyce's *Ulysses*. He drew certain inferences about their personalities and affective states based upon the frequency of occurrence of various of our measures. Although his method was flawed in a number of respects, Steinberg showed that the literary critic's work can be enriched by close attention to aspects of style associated with grammatical structures.

We can approach the analysis of written communication in one of two ways: (1) by establishing norms and redoing the various clinical investigations already performed on spoken language or (2) by comparing free speech and free writing directly. If we can show that our categories appear with approximately equal frequency in spoken and written messages, we are justified in assuming that our method is suitable for the analysis of free writing.

Vygotsky on Spoken and Written Language

Some of the most penetrating remarks about the relationship between speech and writing were stated by Vygotsky over 40 years ago (1962). The Russian psychologist's notions grew out of his attempt to understand the complex connections between thought and language. His analysis included motivational, conceptual, and structural factors.

Vygotsky began by trying to account for the well-known fact that children find writing far more difficult than speaking. Children, he pointed out, are not highly motivated to write because their needs cannot be satisfied quickly in that way. The listener usually is present and able to respond immediately to a spoken request; the reader generally is absent or, if present, incapable of a rapid reply.

Writing is more difficult than speaking, argued Vygotsky, because it requires more detachment. Writing is speech "without an interlocutor. . . . In written speech we are obliged to create the situation, to represent it to ourselves. . . . This demands detachment from the actual situation" (p. 99). Speakers can convey part of their meaning by gestures, variations in intonational contours, and so on. The writer, on the other hand, must explain the situation fully in order to be understood by the reader. Written messages, therefore, are more fully deployed syntactically than spoken ones.

Since speakers can transmit messages in nonverbal ways, Vygotsky believed that written communication required a much greater number of words than speech to convey the same idea. With respect to syntactic differentiation, he placed oral speech between the more abbreviated inner speech and the fully deployed written form.

Recent Comparisons of Speaking and Writing

A small but growing number of publications comparing spoken and written communication has been accumulating during the past 15 years. Sociolinguists and psychologists have demonstrated a number of significant differences between the two modes of verbal expression. Let us review this literature briefly before describing our own experimental work.

Investigators agree that speech takes less effort and therefore is more productive per unit of time (Blass & Siegman, 1975; Davis & Taft, 1976; Horowitz & Berkowitz, 1964; Horowitz & Newman, 1964). Although innate neuromuscular mechanisms undoubtedly play an important part in the relative degree of ease associated with speaking and writing, other factors also have been noted. Children learn to speak early in life in a natural and spontaneous way. Speech is self-taught and only requires interaction with speaking persons. All children born free of physical and psychological impairments will learn to understand and speak the language of their society, with or without formal education. Writing, on the other hand, must be taught systematically. There are no known maturational processes leading to the natural acquisition of writing skills.

Vygotsky's assertion that writing requires more words than speaking to convey the same ideas has not been confirmed by researchers. In a carefully designed study comparing free speech and free writing among a group of college students, Horowitz & Newman (1964) found writing to be more deliberate and economical. Although spoken communications produced more ideas per unit of time, due to a more elevated rate, written messages contained more ideas per number of words.

Speaking has been described as possessing more psychological freedom because, in contrast to writing, it creates no permanent record. A speaker can "take back" a remark or deny having said it; a written statement is not subject to this kind of correction (Horowitz & Newman, 1964). We do not know if the electronic recording of speech makes it less "free"; the problem, to our knowledge, has not been addressed systematically.

Speech has been characterized as expressive and impulsive, writing as more intellectual, rational, and formal. We cannot ignore the effect of immediate feedback on the verbal behavior of speakers. The continuous verbal and nonverbal reactions of the listener are powerful encouraging or deterring social influences upon the behavior of the speaker. We may attribute, in part, the greater productivity of speech to the inability of most people to tolerate silence.

Writing is more autonomous than speaking and, despite the resulting permanent record, may allow for deviations from social norms. We would expect such deviations to be affected by the degree to which the writer is known to the reader. Anonymous speakers often are extraordinarily free of customary social restraints.

With respect to grammar, most investigators have supported Vygotsky's observation that written messages are syntactically more complex than spoken ones. Writers, for example, have been said to use more subordinate and modifying clauses than speakers (Harrell, 1957). One researcher has described oral language as "less abstract" than written communication and as containing more finite verbs and fewer nouns of abstraction (DeVito, 1967). A higher verb-to-adjective ratio has been reported in speech, whereas writing supposedly contains longer words. A recent study concluded that "in relation to oral systems, written systems were more complex in structure; revealed more adjectival but less adverbial elaboration;

showed more complex verb structures; but contained fewer indices of personal reference" (Poole & Field, 1976).

Situational variables may reinforce differentially the use of speaking and writing. In school, teachers often encourage and praise written communication but may forbid and punish talking under certain circumstances (Davis & Taft, 1976). Because of its greater rapidity, speaking allows less time than writing for the planning and encoding of messages. This undoubtedly contributes to the greater redundancy of spoken communication (Horowitz & Newman, 1964).

Our speech can be modified by vocal mannerisms, facial expressions, and gestures. It is true that handwriting also reveals personality, but the average reader is less sensitive to paralinguistic variables associated with writing than most listeners are to a speaker's nonverbal behavior. This difference in sensitivity probably is due to the different ways we learn to speak and to write. Speech is acquired very early in life at a time when communication between mother and child is saturated with nonverbal signals. We learn the intonational patterns and gestures accompanying spoken language long before we can understand the meaning of the words themselves. Writing, on the other hand, is learned in a more affectively neutral setting, long after we have acquired the basic phonological, syntactic, and semantic structures of our native tongue.

Finally, since we learn to speak at home and to write at school, individual variations in writing are more apt to be related to formal educational opportunities than are differences in speaking.

Problems of Method in Studies Comparing Speech and Writing

Of the various differences between speaking and writing reported in the literature, we believe that only the greater rapidity of speech has been established clearly. Investigators reporting grammatical differences between the two modes of communication have not paid sufficient attention to experimental variables that may have biased their results in a certain direction.

Vygotsky (1962) stressed the effects upon the syntactic elaboration of written and spoken language of (1) the relationship of the writer to the reader and (2) the opportunities for nonverbal communication between speaker and listener. Most studies comparing speech and writing have not controlled adequately for the role of the experimenter.

Investigators of speech and writing often have gathered the two sets of data by means of different stimuli. DeVito (1967), for example, who reported oral language to be significantly less abstract than written language, compared samples of articles written by college professors with oral comments made by the same professors about their articles. Poole & Field (1976), who also found greater syntactic complexity in the writing samples of college students, collected their spoken material during individual recording sessions and their written productions in a group setting. To complicate matters further, Poole & Field used two sets of instructions to collect their oral and written samples. The speakers were presented structured interview schedules that contained questions on secondary-school and university experiences; the writers were asked simply to foretell the story of their lives from the time of leaving school until retirement.

The most carefully controlled study comparing speech and writing, in our judgment, was conducted by Horowitz & Newman (1964). They asked 2 groups of 20 college students to write or speak on 2 topics: "What does a good teacher mean to you?" and "What does a good citizen mean to you?" Twenty students spoke on one subject and wrote on the other; the other 20 students reversed the procedure. Order of presentation was controlled for. Although Horowitz & Newman found spoken expression to be more repetitious and productive per unit of time, they presented no data to support the notion that writing is more "abstract" or syntactically more complex than speech.

Comparing Free Speech and Free Writing

Our summary of recent studies comparing speech and writing suggests that no firm conclusions about syntactic differences between the two modes of communication are justified. All investigations showing grammatical differences between oral and written expression had serious procedural flaws.

We decided to compare free writing and free speech by applying our method of verbal behavior analysis in the usual nondirective and unstructured way. We wished to ascertain, first of all, if our verbal mechanisms appear with approximately equal frequency in spoken and written samples. We also were interested in the degree to which a given individual used a similar grammatical style when speaking and writing. We reasoned that if our categories were equally represented in oral and written productions and if a given individual used similar syntactic devices for speaking and writing, we would be justified in applying our method to written messages.

We collected free-speech and free-writing samples from a group of 14 medical students. The students were unfamiliar with the goals and strategies of our investigation. They simply were told that they would be asked to write or speak during 2 experimental sessions separated by an interval of 1 week. Although we can assume that the students were an intelligent, well-educated group, they were drawn from a wide variety of socioeconomic and ethnic backgrounds. Each volunteer provided a 10-minute sample of spontaneous speech, collected according to the method described in Chapter 2, and 5 pages of free writing. The written samples were gathered by asking each subject to write on any topic or topics she wished until 5 pages of 8" × 11" lined composition paper were filled.[1] In order to control for the effect of order, we had half the subjects speak the first week and write the second week; the other half completed the 2 tasks in reverse order.

The samples were scored for 13 of the 14 categories described in Chapter 2. We did not calculate long pauses because of the technical difficulties involved in monitoring subjects' writing behavior.[2] A 2-factor analysis of variance with repeated measures on 1 factor was performed for mode of communication and order in the 13 categories. Table 6–1 shows that in only 2 categories did we find significant differences between the speaking and writing samples. The volunteers had a higher rate and used more qualifiers when talking. No significant order effect was found.

We thus were able to confirm the finding of Horowitz & Newman (1964) that free speech is more productive per unit of time than free writing. All subjects spoke at least twice as rapidly as they wrote; the mean speaking rate was 5 times that of the speed of writing. We must keep in mind that comparisons of total productivity were rendered meaningless by our strategy of limiting the period of speaking to 10 minutes, while requiring a certain amount of written material without limitations of time.

The volunteers' less frequent use of qualifiers when writing is attributable in part to experimental variables. Since there were no time limits to the writing part of the procedure, they had more time to plan and encode messages. Speakers often use qualifiers to fill pauses while planning more definitive statements. In the presence of an experimenter, the pressure to speak without interruption was undoubtedly much greater than the need to maintain an unbroken stream of written messages. Other investigators also have reported speech to be more loose and vague than writing (Horowitz & Newman, 1964).

Our data show that only 1 of 10 categories related to grammatical structures distinguished the spoken from the written samples. We believe that this is further evidence that our categories measure stable linguistic habits. It is possible, of course, that we would have

Table 6–1. Comparison of Medical Students' Written and Spoken Language: Mean; (S.E.M.).

Category	Written Samples		Spoken Samples		F	r
Words	1015.5	(54.6)	1117.1	(131.4)	2.14	0.21
Rate	22.1	(1.8)	119.3	(11.3)	88.95†	0.71†
Direct References	3.0	(0.7)	1.6	(0.3)	2.89	−0.13
Nonpersonal References	587.4	(52.9)	590.1	(41.6)	< 1.0	0.40
I	40.6	(4.8)	47.5	(6.6)	1.23	0.41
We	5.7	(1.8)	5.6	(2.0)	< 1.0	−0.04
Me	5.3	(0.9)	7.1	(1.3)	1.48	0.18
Qualifiers	8.1	(0.9)	14.9	(1.9)	13.75†	0.34
Retractors	7.3	(0.6)	7.0	(0.9)	< 1.0	0.48*
Feelings	5.4	(1.1)	6.1	(1.4)	< 1.0	0.52*
Evaluators	14.3	(2.8)	13.5	(2.1)	< 1.0	0.74†
Negatives	15.4	(2.5)	18.2	(2.2)	2.33	0.70†
Explainers	6.8	(0.8)	8.0	(1.4)	< 1.0	0.15

*$p < .05$ (one-tailed)
†$p < .01$ (two-tailed)

found more significant differences between free speech and free writing had we used more complex categories. We suspect that measures involving the use of subordinate, embedded clauses would appear more frequently in written samples since they require additional time for planning and encoding. In any case, the findings lend encouragement to the hope that verbal systems such as ours can be applied usefully to the analysis of written material.

We were not able to confirm certain findings reported by other investigators. Spoken language has been said, by Horowitz & Newman (1964) for example, to include more feeling and impulsivity and less "of the intellectualized and rational" person. Our data, however, show no significant differences between writing and speaking in the categories of expressions of feeling, retractors, and explainers. Since Horowitz & Newman presented no data to support their conclusions, further comparisons between our results and their observations are not possible.

Poole & Field (1976) reported that, compared to speech, written language contains "fewer indices of personal reference." Again, our data do not support these findings, since we found no significant differences in the nonpersonal references and personal pronouns categories. Most likely, differences in category construction and data collection account for the lack of congruent findings. We have noted already that Poole & Field gathered their spoken and written samples under widely differing experimental conditions. Their results therefore must be interpreted with extreme caution.

Intrasubject Comparisons of Speech and Writing

If the volunteers showed few differences between their speaking and writing styles when examined as a group, what can we say about their consistency when considered individually? We correlated scores for each category, based upon written and spoken modes of testing for the 14 subjects, using a Pearson product–moment correlation. Table 6–1 shows that significant associations were obtained in 5 of the 13 categories: expressions of feeling, negatives, rate of speech, evaluators, and retractors. We were encouraged that as many as 5 categories related to grammatical structures showed significant intra-individual consistency, particularly in view of the small number of subjects in the study.

Subjects' Differential Reactions to the Stresses of Free Speech and Free Writing

The content of the transcripts, as well as remarks directed to the experimenter by certain volunteers after the procedure, suggested to us that a number of subjects approached the speaking and writing parts of the experiment with different expectations. Several volunteers who had little trouble speaking spontaneously were able to produce 5 pages of free writing only with great difficulty. Believing that their ability to compose creatively and with style would be judged by the experimenter, these subjects picked formal, impersonal topics for their written samples, while speaking more informally about personal life experiences. Other volunteers had the opposite problem. They wrote easily and spontaneously but seemed awed by the prospect of speaking extemporaneously for 10 minutes. These subjects also allayed their anxiety by choosing safe, impersonal topics about which to talk. The following excerpts will give the reader an idea of how certain volunteers grappled with the challenge of filling 5 pages with free writing or speaking spontaneously for 10 minutes.

One student provided 10 minutes of free speech during the first week of the experiment. He completed the task rather easily and made no complaint to the experimenter about the procedure. When asked to provide 5 pages of free writing the following week, he began in the following manner:

> I really dislike this part of your experiment because writing for me is a sacred challenge. It's deliberate, throughout, and supposedly has a thread of continuity. Free association in ink is OK, I guess, but I think it depresses me more than most things do. I try to make sure that I'm not blocking anything by sitting silent for however long it takes to feel like I've infused what I'm feeling into thoughts. After that comes the art of architecture. I feel like I can't do that here. . . . Perhaps by the time I get to the fifth side, I'll decide that I don't give a damn about your interest in this and do what I feel like.

Another subject, who found writing an easier task than talking, began speaking as follows:

Are my ten minutes up? I'm rambling because I want my 10 minutes to be up. . . . I'm really interested in what the analysis of this tape might be and I would appreciate knowing the results of the experiment and etc. etc. etc. Um, OK, um. . . . How much time do I have? Is it 5 more minutes, 3, 2, 6? Ha, ha, ha! Well, it's amazing that for a formal experiment of this type, the passage of time could be slowed so because I would swear that I've been in here 10 minutes.

One week later, the same volunteer began the written portion of the procedure by stating:

Having completed the tape recorded portion of this experiment, I can now utilize the manner of communication with which I feel most comfortable. Beginning the experiment [i.e., the free-speech portion] evoked some mysterious anxiety in me. What was I to discuss? How would it sound? Would my speech be a true reflection of how I thought and felt? Would the image evoked by my speech be different from my own image of myself? If so, then what was that image? Immediately after beginning the experiment, after I had spoken the first few phrases, I felt even more wary. My speech sounded distant and formal, as if I were posing. Thinking about it further worsened my anxiety. . . . Writing not only allows me fulfilling social communication but also satisfactory encounters with myself. On the other hand, speech as a mode of communication often unsettles me, it requires more psychic effort with less positive feedback.

We can see from these excerpts how individuals may be stressed to different degrees by free writing and free speaking. In our judgment, this factor more than any other accounts for the failure of our volunteers to achieve positive intra-individual correlations in all categories.

Certain investigators of speaking and writing behavior have commented upon the preferences of subjects for one or the other mode of expression. One published report emphasized the importance of considering subjects' "natural felicity" for writing and speaking when interpreting research data (Horowitz & Newman, 1964). In a recent study of Australian secondary-school students, preference for speaking over writing was reported to correlate positively "with sociability and with the quality of oral expression." According

to the authors, "a preference for speaking may arise from the enjoyment of the company of people, but where this enjoyment is limited,
or where oral competence is poor, a person will prefer to communicate in writing (Davis & Taft, 1976). All experienced teachers know
that many students who are excellent writers are not comfortable
participating in classroom discussions; indeed, they may become
flustered and inarticulate if forced to do so. The opposite is also true:
effective speakers often are surprisingly incompetent when asked to
put their thoughts on paper.

With respect to our own study, we believe that certain modifications of our method might bring the results of the writing
portion of the procedure closer in line with those of the speaking
part. A time limit for writing the 5 pages, for example, would put the
volunteers under the same kind of pressure they experience when
speaking for 10 minutes. Since our subjects wrote about one-fifth as
quickly as they spoke, a 45-minute period to complete 5 pages of
writing might be appropriate. We believe it also would be helpful to
encourage writers to ignore concerns about grammatical form.

Much additional research will be required to determine which
forms of written expression are most revealing of personality. There
is already some experimental work indicating that the more formal
the writing task required, the fewer grammatical differences there
are among subjects. Robinson (1965) found significant syntactic
differences between British middle-class and working-class children's writing samples when they were asked to pen informal letters. Most of the differences disappeared when the children wrote
formal letters. We believe that studies like Robinson's tend to
vindicate our strategy of requiring free writing samples of our volunteers rather than discussions of suggested topics. In writing, as in
speaking, the less structured the experimental procedure, the more
varied the responses.

Speech Patterns and Educational Background

In general, our volunteers performed similarly in the spoken and
written parts of the experiment. Was this due in part to their high
level of education? Can we assume that subjects with less formal

education would perform in comparable ways? Although little experimental work has been done in this area, there are some indications in published reports of a positive relationship between pro-
ficiency in speaking and competence in writing, which could affect
performance in the categories we measure (Loban, 1963).

In order to see what effects, if any, educational achievement
might have on the use of our categories, we decided to compare the
speech samples of the 14 medical students with those of 23 male
members of the U.S. Army and Air Force between the ages of 18 and
45. We described this group of subjects in great detail in Chapters 2
and 3. The reader will recall that the armed forces volunteers were
drawn from a variety of occupations and had, on the average, a
high-school education.

We compared scores cf the medical students' performance in
each of 12 categories against those of the military volunteers, using a
t test with a correction for unequal variance. (Long pauses and rate
of speech were not computed.) Our results showed that the medical
students scored significantly higher than the armed-forces subjects
in 4 categories: (1) qualifiers, (2) nonpersonal references, (3) evaluators, and (4) the pronoun, *me*. Considered together, these findings suggest that, compared to the military controls, the students
were more tentative, passive, impersonal, and concerned with
questions of morality and propriety. The verbal pattern reflects a
style of speaking generally associated with obsessional character
traits (Lorenz, 1955).

We should note that tentative expressions and impersonal,
passive constructions also have been associated with syntactical
maturity (Loban, 1963), a possible consequence of increased educational achievement. Differences between the two groups, therefore, might be due in part to differences in educational background.
The reader will recall, however, that we were unable to demonstrate in any of the four categories higher frequencies as a function of
increasing age and education in our study of children and adolescents reported in Chapter 3. It is probable, therefore, that personality differences accounted for most of the contrast in verbal styles
between the medical students and the armed-forces volunteers. We
cannot exclude as a confounding factor the likely positive association
between compulsivity and scholastic achievement.

Summary

We compared a group of male medical students' free speech and free writing and found that almost all verbal mechanisms used in our system appeared with equal frequency in the two modes of expression. In only 2 of the 13 categories we measured, rate of speech and qualifiers, did significant differences appear, and the first can be accounted for partly on the basis of neuromuscular mechanisms. We conclude, therefore, that our method is applicable to the analysis of free writing.

Intrasubject comparisons indicated that in about half the categories related to syntactical variables, consistency of performance prevailed. Where stable performance was not present, we could attribute the results to the fact that the volunteers were not stressed equally by the two experimental tasks, certain subjects finding writing an easier challenge, others preferring speaking. We believe that we can compensate for this difficulty by modifying the instructions in certain respects.

When we compared the speech samples of the medical students with those of normal armed forces volunteers having fewer years of formal education, we found significant differences in 4 of 12 categories. The results were consistent with the assumption that individuals choosing careers in medicine tend to demonstrate certain obsessional qualities in their spoken language. We cannot, however, exclude the possibility that some of the differences were related to greater syntactical maturity among the more educated students.

The clinical study of written language, particularly its grammatical features, has received less systematic attention than the investigation of speech. We believe this is due to the fact that psychiatric diagnosis and treatment are carried out largely through the medium of spoken language. The data we presented in this chapter suggest that close attention to written documents will be rewarded amply by increased clinical understanding of the writer.

Notes

1. We assumed that, for most subjects, 5 pages of 8″ × 11″ paper would contain approximately 1000 words.

2. A male experimenter was alone in the room with the volunteer and carefully recorded the amount of time spent completing the task. There was no time limit.

Chapter 7
The Grammatical Reflections of Anger

Controversy Regarding Verbal Communication of Affect

No problem in communications research is more vexing than the identification of the ways in which we express feelings. Although few well-designed studies have been carried out in this area, most investigators assume that emotions are transmitted primarily through nonverbal channels. Like many beliefs lacking firm experimental support, this particular bias has been argued with vigor by a number of authors.

Researchers and clinicians have used three principal lines of reasoning to minimize the importance of verbalization in emotional exchanges. While the first two are little more than appeals to common sense, the third does have the backing of several well-executed studies. The arguments run as follows:

(1) Since affective messages undoubtedly are exchanged between mother and infant during preverbal stages of child development, nonverbal signals, in the form of facial expressions, gestures, and vocalizations, are presumed to be the principal modes of emotional expression throughout life (Moskowitz, 1978).

(2) Investigators working with congenitally deaf children raised by deaf parents have reported that such children can grow into normal adults, free of significant personality defects. Vernon & Miller (1973) have taken these reports to be "overwhelming

evidence against assigning a primary role to verbal language in affective development." After briefly and selectively surveying the literature, these authors have concluded that, with respect to speech, "affect is transmitted not through verbal language but by means less subject to conscious control—in this case the voice quality."

(3) Mahl (1956) and others have demonstrated positive associations between experimentally induced states of anxiety and such nonverbal speech disruptions as incoherent sounds, sentence incompletions, and stuttering. Even more convincing have been studies showing that filtered, content-free speech can communicate feelings reliably by means of such paralinguistic variables as tone, volume, rate, and rhythm (Milmoe et al., 1967; Starkweather, 1956).

We believe that the arguments just presented are persuasive but far from conclusive. It is true that an infant can have affective exchanges with its mother before it can understand verbal signals, but that does not mean that words play no communicative role during the first few months of life. Long before they begin to speak, children are familiar with the intonation contours of their mother tongue. Although mother's words may not be understood, they undoubtedly play a role in molding these contours, which form the basis of future syntactic development. A child can produce declarative, interrogative, and imperative sentences before he can utter recognizable words, solely from sounds marked by differing stress and intonational patterns. In a sense, he already can understand and speak the adult language of his society before he knows the meaning of a single word (Menyuk, 1969).

The assertion that congenitally deaf children raised by deaf parents can develop free of significant psychopathology proves only that for these individuals adequate emotional exchange with others can occur without verbal messages. In our judgment, it says nothing about the role of speech in the socialization of children with normal hearing. One might as well contend that hands are not important for writing because individuals not having them can be taught to write with their feet. Vernon & Miller (1973) are not consistent in their reasoning since they do attribute to nonverbal vocalizations, a channel not available to the congenitally deaf, an important role in the transmission of affective messages.

Not all clinicians agree that the congenitally deaf usually grow into adulthood free of serious ego defects. Edelheit (1969), in his discussion of the relationship of speech and psychic structure, has written that deaf children "are severely hampered in their development" because of their impaired capacity for verbalization. Political controversies concerning the relative merits of teaching verbal versus nonverbal language skills to the deaf, unfortunately, have influenced the clinical judgment and theoretical biases of investigators in the field.

Finally, without knowing what the relationship may be between mental representations of word symbols and phonological syntactic structures, we cannot be sure that content-free speech does not stimulate in the mind of the listener corresponding verbal signals. Just as a melody brings to mind the familiar lyrics, the pitch modulation conveyed in content-free speech may evoke memories of appropriate words.

Investigators who belittle the importance of verbal content in the expression of feelings seem to forget that poets have been successfully stirring the emotions of readers for thousands of years. Although rhythm, rhyme, alliteration, and other devices undoubtedly contribute to poetry's evocative effect, much of the poet's success lies in the skillful use of semantic and syntactic aspects of manifest verbal content. If words could not move a reader, who would bother to write a love letter or a suicide note?

Committed to the primacy of paralanguage in the communication of affects, Mahl (1963) nevertheless has recognized that grammatical constructions can be useful indicators of emotions. Davitz & Davitz (1959), who have studied the transmission of affects by content-free speech also have allowed for the possibility that the structure of language might be associated with particular feelings.

The relationship of verbal style and affect has been noted by certain students of communication. Ruesch & Prestwood (1949), for example, have observed that excited speakers use many feeling words, personal pronouns, and subjective qualifications. When relaxed, they employ fewer of these structures and more concrete nouns and objective qualifications. Anger, according to these authors, is characterized by an increase in expressions of "self-instigated" action.

Edelson (1975) recently has stressed the close association of syntactic structures and emotions. He has written, "Knowledge of how deployment of particular linguistic resources evokes emotive meaning is essential to the psychoanalyst's interpretation of an analysand's affects" (p. 89).

In a sense, we undertook the task of describing affective speech when we studied a group of depressed, psychiatric inpatients in Chapter 4. The reader will recall that the depressed patients differed from a group of normal controls in a number of verbal categories. They spoke fewer words, had a slower rate, paused more frequently, used the pronouns "I" and "me" more often, made fewer nonpersonal references, and had higher direct references, negatives, and evaluators scores. Depression, however, may include a variety of emotions, such as sadness, hopelessness, helplessness, and often guilt and anxiety. We do not know which of our verbal findings can be associated with specific feelings found in depression. Another consideration is the fact that depression often develops in predisposed individuals. It is possible, therefore, that certain of the speech aberrations we found existed already in the premorbid condition as trait-dependent characteristics. Investigators have begun to distinguish trait from situational anxiety, and it may be necessary to approach other emotions in the same manner (Dibner, 1956).

Steinberg (1973), in his rather free-wheeling application of our system to the characters of James Joyce's *Ulysses*, noted certain changes in the formal characteristics of Molly's speech when she became sexually aroused. According to Steinberg, her use of qualifiers, retractors, and negatives decreased, the latter being replaced by more affirmative words and expressions. Although Joyce's characters are fictional, their long monologues undoubtedly were influenced by what Joyce heard in real-life situations.

Methodological Problems in the Experimental Investigation of Emotions

Clinical and fictional reporting of "emotional speech" is one thing; the systematic study of affective messages is quite another. If identifying speech styles associated with patterns of behavior is difficult, the experimental investigation of affects presents us with a number of procedural problems that have not yet been resolved satisfactorily.

Defining and identifying clinically significant patterns of behavior is relatively easy. Constructing categories that can capture and reflect the characteristic coping mechanisms of deviant populations, although more challenging, presents no insurmountable problems. The categories then can be validated readily by stressing volunteers under controlled laboratory conditions. We can assume that whatever verbal styles emerge are representative of general patterns of thinking and behaving. Emotions, on the other hand, are mercurial, transient, difficult to provoke, and almost impossible to capture for purposes of investigation.

Researchers working in the area of affective display have had to face two distinct but closely related procedural problems: (1) How may a feeling be defined so that independent judges can agree on its outward manifestations? and (2) How can experimental subjects be made to experience and transmit emotions over a long enough period of time so that the various verbal and nonverbal characteristics associated with these affects can be recorded in the laboratory? Investigators have proposed a number of strategies to deal with these methodological problems. We may consider them under three headings: suggesting emotions to experimental subjects; using electronically produced sounds; and sampling natural conversations.

Suggesting Emotions to Experimental Subjects

A common and simple strategy, one used by Davitz & Davitz (1959), is to ask volunteers to try to convey, under experimental conditions, a suggested emotion. Davitz & Davitz, who were studying the communication of feelings by content-free speech, asked their subjects to express requested feelings while reciting the alphabet. Other subjects, acting as judges, then attempted to determine the quality of the feelings expressed. Certain researchers have used hypnosis to suggest specific emotions to experimental subjects (Zuckerman, et al., 1964).

Because individuals differ greatly among themselves in their ability to express feelings, certain investigators have employed trained actors who are supposedly expert in the art of communicating a wide variety of emotions (Fairbanks & Hoaglin, 1941; Feldstein, 1964).

Clinical investigators have placed subjects in anxiety-stimulating situations, such as stress interviews (Kasl & Mahl, 1965; Lalljee & Cook, 1975; Siegman & Pope, 1965), or in anger-provoking situations (Zuckerman et al, 1964; Shope, Hedrick, & Green, 1978), where they have been subjected to planned frustrations or physical punishment. Less extreme techniques have included showing volunteers emotional films or having them read provocative articles.

Electronically Produced Sounds

Researchers have used electronically produced sounds to convey "feelings" by varying pitch, amplitude, tempo, and signal duration. Scherer (1974), for example, employed artificial stimuli produced by a Moog synthesizer "to assess more precisely the way in which inferences of emotional content are based on specific acoustic cues and their combinations." He found that judges were influenced most by tempo and pitch variations.

As we might have expected, simulated or artificial "feelings" have been dismissed by certain investigators as not comparable to genuine emotions, or, as stated by one author, "the validity of the assumed equivalency between simulated emotions and those manifested in affective states [has] not been demonstrated. (Natale, 1977).

Sampling Natural Discourse

At the cost of some methodological rigor, we may study feelings in less contrived ways, by sampling natural conversations, psychotherapy sessions, initial psychological interviews, and so on (Dibner, 1956; Pope & Siegman, 1962). By recruiting subjects predisposed to the transmission of certain affects, we can focus on those feelings of particular concern to us. An experimenter interested in studying anxiety, for example, can administer a screening device, such as the

Taylor Manifest Anxiety Test, to a large number of volunteers and select those with the highest scores (Benton, Hartman, & Sarason, 1955). The chosen subjects' speech then can be sampled in one of a variety of natural settings.

Emotions and Action Language

Even when independent judges agree on the outward manifestations of a specific emotion, we can never be certain that the perceived affect corresponds to what the experimental subject actually feels. No measureable responses, including autonomic nervous system reactions, provide us with the specificity we seek. Investigators have questioned seriously whether a state of physiological arousal is sufficient to induce a specific emotion. Schachter & Singer (1962), for example, have contended that the state of physiological arousal accompanying a feeling is relatively nonspecific. According to these authors, "Cognitions arising from the immediate situations as interpreted by past experience provide the framework within which one understands and labels his feelings. It is the cognition which determines whether the state of physiological arousal will be labeled as 'anger,' 'joy,' 'fear,' or whatever." Schachter & Singer believe that neither a state of arousal nor cognitive circumstances alone are sufficient to indicate an emotion; both are required.

In general, researchers have been content to accept the verdict of judges as to the genuineness of a feeling they are asked to identify. In our present state of knowledge, we are unable to measure with greater certainty something as ephemeral as a feeling.

Since we are studying speech as behavior, the reader may wonder why we have not eliminated the "ghost in the machine" (Ryle, 1965) by refraining from the use of such terms as "emotions," "feelings," "affective states," and so on. Why do we not simply limit ourselves to a description of outwardly observable behavior and not attempt to infer the presence of unverifiable internal states? There is a good deal to be said for the exclusive use of the kind of action language proposed by Schafer (1976), but we believe such a practice to be grammatically awkward; it also would suggest a bias that we do not share entirely.

Specificity of Emotions

We by no means have exhausted the procedural problems inherent in the study of affective states. Feelings, unfortunately, lack the discreteness desirable for laboratory study, for the receiver as well as for the sender. Judges cannot distinguish easily between certain emotions that appear to be quite different, such as love and sadness (Davitz & Davitz, 1959). Affects like anger, on the other hand, seemingly are perceived more easily.

Another complicating factor is the broad range of phenomena comprised by most terms used to designate emotions. "Anger," which generally is considered to be one of the easier feelings to identify, may include unrestrained shouting, smoldering resentment, and sarcasm. Even the most clear-cut emotions become elusive when examined closely. We shall make little progress in the study of affects until we define more carefully than heretofore what it is we are measuring.

Investigators interested in the relationship between affective states and verbal style have the additional problem of maintaining a feeling state in their volunteers long enough to permit the monitoring of infrequently occurring speech phenomena. Most of the variables measured by our categories appear about 5 to 15 times per 1000 words, yet few experimental subjects can experience and communicate an emotion with any degree of intensity for longer than a minute or two. We believe this to be true for both spontaneous and simulated feelings. Paralinguists are less concerned about the duration of affective display, since they can collect sufficient data for their purposes in extremely brief periods of time.

Speech Pattern Associated with Explosive Anger

We now shall describe a study the purpose of which was to begin to identify and describe some of the syntactical cues associated with the transmission of certain well-defined emotions. We decided for two reasons to launch the study of affective states with explosive, shouting anger. First of all, investigators studying the transmission of emotions agree that anger is one of the more easily communicated feelings (Fairbanks & Hoaglin, 1941; Davitz & Davitz, 1959). Secondly, we assumed that spontaneously occurring angry outbursts would be relatively easy to record during the many diagnostic and therapeutic interviews conducted on the various psychiatric services of the University of Maryland. Many of the psychotherapists in training regularly record individual and family therapy sessions and we believed that collecting appropriate samples of angry behavior would present no great difficulty. We were dismayed to discover that naturally occurring, shouting anger is extremely uncommon in conventional forms of psychotherapy. A survey of all recorded psychotherapy, including sessions held at the University of Maryland Violence Clinic, revealed not a single patient (or therapist!) in a shouting angry state. It is possible, of course, that both patients and therapists were inhibited in their expression of extreme feelings by the knowledge that they were being recorded. In any case, we alerted the clinical faculty and house staff to our need and approximately six months later were informed that a brief course of family therapy, involving an explosively angry young man, had been videotaped. We monitored the recorded material and were able to confirm the existence of numerous, brief temper outbursts. Although the "angry segments" were long enough for the study of vocal dynamics and body language, they were too brief for the measurement of infrequently occurring speech mannerisms. The short bursts of explosive anger did focus our attention, however, on several heretofore unnoticed verbal habits, which led us to create several new categories.

Use of Paid Actors to Simulate Angry States

In view of the difficulties we encountered in trying to obtain long segments of naturally occurring, angry speech, we decided to resort to one of the strategies we described earlier in the chapter. After some reflection, we concluded that the use of paid actor-volunteers offered us the best hope of collecting extended samples of simulated, explosive anger. We contacted the Drama Department of the

University of Maryland, Baltimore County, and hired two young acting students, a man and a woman.

We began by asking each actor-volunteer to provide us with samples of "natural" and "angry" speech. We collected the data in the manner described in Chapter 2; that is, the volunteers were asked to speak without interruption on the subject or subjects of their choice for 10 minutes. The only additional instructions they received was that a "natural" or "shouting angry" feeling be conveyed during the monologue, the experimenter indicating in each case which emotion was to be expressed.

After several recordings, it became clear to us that some procedural modification would be necessary. The actor-subjects simply were unable to behave in an explosively angry manner for as long as 10 minutes. After 2 or 3 minutes, both actors began to sound sad rather than angry. They confirmed our impressions and stated that they actually *felt* depressed after speaking angrily for several minutes. The actors complained that they could not sustain an angry mood for very long unless they had something concrete about which to be angry. As actors, both volunteers considered the experimental task an interesting challenge. The female actor-subject tried to evoke an angry mood by imagining hypothetical or real past incidents of frustration and humiliation. She was most successful when she could become indignant over personal mistreatment. The male actor used the strategy of simulating anger at the experimenter, an approach that caused both participants to feel uncomfortable.

We decided to reduce drastically the length of time of each sample and to provide the actors with imaginary, anger-provoking situations not related to their personal lives. The volunteers assured us that they could speak in an explosively angry way for as many 2-minute segments as we required, providing suitable topics were suggested. They also indicated that they could provide as many brief samples of "natural" speech as needed, with or without suggested topics.

New Categories

On the basis of the performance of the young, explosive patient treated in family therapy, we created four new categories. Although related to formal characteristics of speech, these new categories appeared to have a more rapid rate of change than the variables used in our earlier studies. We scored the following:

1. The personal pronoun, "you," when appearing alone or as part of a contraction. We count both singular and plural forms.
2. All interrogative sentences.
3. All imperatives.
4. All clauses containing profanities.

Collecting "Natural" and "Angry" Speech Samples

The actor-subjects met individually with a male experimenter in the speech laboratory for approximately one hour and were asked to speak spontaneously on seven sets of subjects. Each set consisted of a two-minute "natural" segment, followed after a pause of one minute by a two-minute "explosively angry" sample. One minute after the first set was completed, the subject began the second set, and so on, until the seven sets were finished. The experimenter suggested the following topics, in this order:

1. (a) *Natural:* "Shopping at the supermarket."
   (b) *Angry:* "You are standing in the express checkout line at the supermarket, carrying three items. You are in a hurry. Suddenly a customer with a cart full of groceries cuts in front of you."
2. (a) *Natural:* "A drive in the country."
   (b) *Angry:* "You are driving your new car in the country. Another car is tailgating you. After motioning him to stop several times, you are forced to brake suddenly at an intersection. The car behind you crashes into your rear."
3. (a) *Natural:* "Spending a night in a hotel."
   (b) *Angry:* "You arrive late at night at a hotel in a small town where you have already made a reservation. The desk clerk informs you that the hotel is full and that there is no record of your reservation. There is no other hotel within a 50-mile radius."
4. (a) *Natural:* "Eating out in a restaurant."

      (b) *Angry:* "You have been seated at a table in a restaurant for half an hour. Nobody has taken your order. You have an appointment to be somewhere in an hour. A customer walks into the restaurant. The waitress, ignoring you, immediately takes his order."

5. (a) *Natural:* "Taking an examination."

      (b) *Angry:* "You have been told by your professor that you have to make a certain grade on the final examination in order to pass the course. You just make the grade and are then informed that a higher mark than the one you received will be necessary to pass."

6. (a) *Natural:* "Speaking on the telephone."

      (b) *Angry:* "You are waiting to make an urgent call on a public telephone. The person using the phone has already spent 15 minutes gossiping and shows no sign of finishing the conversation."

7. (a) *Natural:* "Taking a walk."

      (b) *Angry:* "Shortly after having had an ingrown toenail removed from the large toe of your right foot, you take a walk with a few acquaintances. One of them steps on your sore toe, causing you great pain. You politely ask the individual to keep his distance. Several minutes later, he steps on your sore toe again."

Controlling for Effects of Dialogue

It surely will have occurred to the reader that in providing "angry" and "natural" samples to the actors, we were asking them to respond to stimuli that were different in another crucial respect. The "angry" instructions not only provided provocative situations but also adversaries whom they could confront in imaginary arguments. The "natural" instructions, on the other hand, did not mention any individuals and therefore did not lead the actors into hypothetical dialogues. We realized that differences found between "angry" and "natural" samples could be attributed not only to changes in affective state but to differences between narrative and dialogue.

    In order to control for the influence of dialogue, we collected seven additional sets of two-minute speech samples from the male actor. (The female volunteer was not available for this part of the study). The experimenter asked the male actor to speak in a "natural" or "explosively angry" way for two minutes, on any subject or subjects he wished. Except for this change in instructions, we followed the same procedure used in the first part of the study. Although the male actor did not display as much anger as he did when confrontation with adversaries was suggested, we had no difficulty distinguishing "angry" from "natural" samples when listening to the recordings.[1]

Formal Characteristics of Angry Speech

For both instructed and uninstructed parts of the experiment, we computed scores for 13 of the 14 categories described in Chapter 2 and for the 4 new categories defined earlier in this chapter. We did not score direct references; the modified instructions required to elicit angry feelings as well as the change from a 10-minute to a 2-minute speech sample made the use of this category of questionable value.

For the male actor, a two-factor analysis of variance (Angry versus Natural X Instructed versus Uninstructed), with repeated measures on both factors, was performed. When interactions were found, a Dunnett *t* test was used to locate differences among means. A similar analysis of variance was used to compare verbal behavior under angry and natural conditions for the two actors under instructed conditions. In categories where the data did not fit the assumptions underlying the use of an analysis of variance, a Fisher-Yates test was used. Statistical analyses were carried out for 17 categories (Tables 7–1 and 7–2).

When the effects of dialogue and individual variations were discounted, we found explosively angry speech to be characterized primarily by a decline in qualifiers, retractors, and *we*, as well as an increase in negatives and *me*. To a lesser extent, we found the angry samples to have fewer nonpersonal references and more interrogatives, imperatives, and profanities. Let us now try to explain some of these results.

Decreased use of qualifiers and retractors. We attribute much of the flexibility of natural speech to the use of qualifiers and retractors. Both constructions express tentativeness; the former before, the latter after the action. Speakers can avoid painful confrontation by qualifying and retracting their remarks. The angry speaker has no wish to protect his adversary. The restraining influences of ambivalence and guilt are melted in the heat of rage. As normal inhibitions are overcome, the use of diplomatic devices decreases.

Decreased use of "we." In their natural samples, the actors usually discussed incidents that included friends and family members. They recalled pleasant memories of shared activities, necessitating the frequent use of *we*. Their angry samples, on the other hand, reflected adversary relationships in which they expressed shared experiences in terms of *I* versus *you*, rather than *we*.

We found a significant intersubject difference in this category, the female volunteer scoring higher than her male colleague. The reason for the difference could be attributed to her choice of more personal topics. During his natural monologues, the male actor sometimes spoke about general, philosophical issues, whereas the female subject talked almost always of incidents that included friends or relatives. When given the topic, "Speaking on the telephone," for example, the male actor discussed the advantages and disadvantages of the telephone as a means of communication. The female volunteer, on the other hand, used the same topic to relate a specific incident in which she was talking on the phone to her boyfriend.

Decreased use of nonpersonal references. The expression of angry feelings tended to elicit more personal themes during both instructed and uninstructed parts of the experiment. Both actor-volunteers limited impersonal, philosophical discussions to their natural segments. Although it is possible to get angry about general matters, the actors reported that specific situations with definite adversaries helped them to mobilize angry feelings.

Increased use of negatives. We should not be surprised to learn that negatives appeared significantly more frequently in the angry segments, considering some of the uses to which they are put in normal discourse. The following excerpts from the transcripts show how the actors used negatives in their imaginary, hostile confrontations:

Table 7–1. Comparison of Angry and Natural Speech, Male Subject.

Category	Uninstructed		Instructed		F Values		
	Angry	Natural	Angry	Natural	Angry/natural	Instructed/Uninstructed	Interaction
Words	438.0 (21.6)	285.5 (10.6)	261.9 (41.8)	290.4 (12.3)	5.08	8.37*	18.21†
Rate	219.0 (10.8)	142.8 (5.3)	136.7 (19.5)	145.2 (6.1)	6.41	8.10*	16.70†
Nonpersonal References	327.6 (55.3)	487.1 (81.9)	191.0 (29.5)	593.7 (72.6)	17.48†	<1.00	3.20
I	60.7 (11.0)	58.4 (6.1)	91.1 (12.7)	45.8 (12.5)	9.70*	<1.00	3.07
Negatives	37.1 (4.1)	17.5 (3.0)	41.6 (8.8)	18.6 (3.9)	25.80†	<1.00	<1.00
Explainers	7.9 (1.4)	6.7 (2.0)	3.3 (1.0)	8.9 (1.8)	<1.00	<1.00	7.59†
Evaluators	12.3 (3.0)	17.3 (3.6)	7.4 (3.2)	19.9 (4.6)	8.57*	<1.00	1.51
	(6 Samples)		(7 Samples)				

Parametric Analyses—Mean (S.E.M.)

Table 7-1 continued

Nonparametric Analyses (percentage of speech samples in which verbal category was used by the subject)

Category	Uninstructed		Instructed	
	Angry	Natural	Angry	Natural
Pauses§	16.7	0.0	71.4	0.0
We	33.3	66.7	14.3	57.1
Me§	100.0	0.0	100.0	0.0
You	50.0	50.0	85.7	14.3
Qualifiers§	16.7	66.7	28.6	100.0
Retractors§	16.7	83.3	0.0	100.0
Feelings§	83.3	16.7	85.7	100.0
Interrogatives	66.7	33.3	100.0	28.6
Profanities‡	50.0	0.0	14.3	14.3
Imperatives§	33.3	0.0	85.7	0.0
	(6 samples)		(7 samples)	

‡Angry versus natural: $p < .05$
§Angry versus natural: $p < .01$
*$p < .05$
†$p < .01$

Table 7–2. Comparison of Angry and Natural Speech, Male and Female Subjects

Category	Parametric Analyses—Mean (S.E.M.)						
	Subject 1 (male)		Subject 2 (female)		F Values		Interaction
	Angry	Natural	Angry	Natural	Angry/Natural	Male/Female	
Words	261.9 (41.8)	290.4 (12.3)	327.9 (19.2)	335.9 (11.5)	< 1.00	7.81*	< 1.00
Rate	136.7 (19.5)	145.2 (6.1)	163.9 (9.6)	167.9 (5.8)	< 1.00	6.96*	< 1.00
Nonpersonal References	191.0 (29.5)	593.7 (72.6)	214.6 (48.2)	629.7 (73.2)	135.23†	< 1.00	< 1.00
I	91.1 (12.7)	45.8 (12.5)	63.2 (5.7)	31.9 (9.4)	9.88*	3.99	< 1.00
Me	26.4 (6.5)	2.5 (0.7)	22.5 (3.8)	3.8 (2.1)	35.79†	< 1.00	< 1.00
You	48.2 (8.1)	7.6 (3.4)	54.9 (10.6)	18.6 (3.7)	59.86†	1.83	< 1.00
Negatives	41.6 (8.8)	18.6 (3.9)	39.4 (6.0)	16.5 (3.7)	8.25*	< 1.00	< 1.00
Explainers	3.3 (1.0)	8.9 (1.8)	7.1 (2.5)	12.9 (1.3)	17.99†	11.09*	< 1.00
Evaluators	7.4 (3.2)	19.9 (4.6)	17.6 (2.5)	16.2 (2.7)	6.99*	< 1.00	5.99*
	(7 samples)		(7 samples)				

Table 7-2 *continued*

Category	Nonparametric Analyses (percentage of speech samples in which verbal category was used by the subject, based upon 7 samples for each condition)			
	Subject 1 (male)		Subject 2 (female)	
	Angry	Natural	Angry	Natural
Pauses‡	71.4	0.0	28.6	0.0
We‡§	14.3	57.1	28.6	100.0
Qualifiers‡	28.6	100.0	28.6	100.0
Retractors‡	0.0	100.0	28.6	100.0
Feelings	85.7	28.6	42.9	71.4
Interrogatives‡	100.0	14.3	100.0	28.6
Profanities‡§	14.3	0.0	85.7	0.0
Imperatives‡	85.7	0.0	100.0	0.0

*p < .05
†p < .01
‡Angry versus natural: p < .01
§Male versus female: p < .05

169

Male actor (hotel scene): I don't care what you say. Look, that's *not* my problem. I *don't* care what your problem was. I *don't* care if you had a fire.

Female actor (supermarket scene): It's *not* right. This is an express line, for Christ's sake! You *can't* come in here with 30 different items. Besides that, you *can't* count. I *don't* care if you have an appointment. I *don't* care if you are in a hurry.

We associate the verbal act of negation with refusal, opposition, and prohibition. Needless to say, such tendencies were more apt to be found in "angry" than in "natural" speech samples.

Increased use of "me." In almost all their angry samples, the actors developed themes of personal mistreatment; something they had a right to was being withheld. This tendency to see themselves as objects of unfair treatment was reflected verbally by an increased use of *me*, as illustrated by the following excerpts:

Male actor (restaurant scene): Hey lady, wait on *me*. . . . Could you please wait on *me*? Would somebody please wait on *me*?

Female actor (driving scene): You've been following *me* for at least five hours. I kept motioning you to stop following *me*. . . . Give *me* your name. . . . Why the fuck were you following *me* so closely?

Increased use of interrogatives. Almost all questions appeared in the angry segments. Most were of a rhetorical, resentful, and self-righteous nature. The actors generally used rhetorical questions to suggest personal mistreatment, as in the following examples:

Male actor (driving scene): What kind of driving is that? What kind, where'd, where'd you learn to drive? . . . What is the problem? What's your problem? What's your problem?

Female actor (restaurant scene): Don't they see me? . . . Don't they like me? . . . What is with him? Is he blind or something?

Increased use of imperatives. The actors used imperatives only in angry samples, usually to demand something from imaginary adversaries. Believing that what they wanted was being wrongfully withheld, the volunteers dispensed with the usual verbal expressions of tact, as indicated in the following excerpts:

Male actor (telephone scene): Hang up! Hang up before I hang up on you!

Female actor (supermarket scene): Put them away! Put them back and get back there in line! Get back in line where you belong!

Increased use of profanities. Not surprisingly, we found expletives more frequently in the angry samples of both actors. Neither volunteer used any profanities in the natural monologues.

The female actor cursed more than the male. Six out of seven of her angry samples contained expletives, whereas the male volunteer cursed in only one of seven monologues. It is likely that cursing is easier for certain individuals than for others. Perhaps the female volunteer was less inhibited than the male in the presence of a male experimenter. Interestingly, other investigators have reported a greater ease on the part of women in expressing verbal aggression (Shope, Hedrick, & Green, 1978).

Speech Pattern Associated with Dialogue

We already have made reference to the fact that simulated dialogue was encouraged by instructions given to the two actors during part one of the experiment. When we examine the results of part two, during which the male volunteer was free to choose his own topics, it is clear that certain of the differences we found between angry and natural samples under instructed conditions can be attributed to imaginary dialogue.

Our data suggest that the use of the following structures is increased by both anger and dialogue:

Personal references. We would expect dialogue to elicit more personal forms of speech than other kinds of communication. This is obvious and requires no additional comment.

Interrogatives. We usually ask questions, even rhetorical ones, of other people: interrogatives are, therefore, more apt to appear in simulated dialogues than in monologues. It is true that our non-directive experimental procedure can be considered a dialogue in which one of the participants is silent. As we reported in Chapters 3 and 4, however, only psychologically deviant or immature speakers direct numerous questions at the experimenter. We regard such a practice as a form of interpersonal regression, an inability to participate in the experiment according to agreed-upon rules.

Imperatives. What we have said about the use of interrogatives applies equally to imperatives. Commands almost always are directed at other individuals, and we would expect their frequency to increase in simulated dialogue. Again, nothing prevented the male actor from commanding the experimenter during part two of the study. Such a strategy, in fact, was used by him in several practice "angry" sessions preceding the experiment. He did not choose to confront the experimenter during the formal procedure.

We observed that certain categories were used more during dialogue but were unrelated to the expression of anger. The pronouns "I" and "you" were used significantly more by the actors during the angry segments of part one of the study. Since no differences emerged in part two, we must attribute the significant findings in part one to the effect of simulated dialogue.

Explainers. The actors used this category less frequently during the angry segments. Explainers, like qualifiers and retractors, can soften the effects of harsh words and actions. Where anger is sufficiently hot, the need for justification declines. Interestingly, we found a significant intersubject difference in this category. The female actor used more explainers than the male, a confirmation of the sex difference we reported in Chapter 2.

Explainers did not distinguish angry from natural speech for the male actor under uninstructed conditions. We cannot offer a convincing reason for this finding. It is possible that discussing an anger-provoking situation in the presence of a neutral experimenter requires justification for one's thoughts and actions. In a hypothetical, explosive encounter, on the other hand, the speaker may ignore the experimenter and feel no need to offer explanations to an imaginary opponent.

Long pauses. Both actors had significantly higher scores in this category under instructed conditions. Neither volunteer had any silences during the natural segments. Although the differences were not significant, the male actor paused more often and for longer periods of time than the female subject. Listening to the recordings, we were impressed that long pauses seemed to occur when the male actor was choking with rage. His anger interfered in some way with the processes of planning, retrieval, and encoding that are necessary for fluent discourse. Curiously, under uninstructed conditions, only one of six of his angry segments contained a long pause. Whether this indicated a lesser degree of anger, or, perhaps, a more articulate response to a broader choice of topics, is unclear.

Syntactic Simplification during Dialogue

Our data strongly suggest that both anger and dialogue are associated with the use of simple grammatical structures. This effect of dialogue upon the formal characteristics of speech has been noted by other students of language. Vygotsky (1962), for example, observed that dialogue is grammatically less complex than monologue. Of the two, he wrote, "monologue is indeed the higher, more complicated form. . . . Dialogue implies immediate unpremeditated utterance. It consists of replies, repartee; it is a chain of reaction. Monologue, by comparison, is a complex formation; the linguistic elaboration can be attended to leisurely" (p. 144).

We can attribute the simplicity of dialogue to the fact that the participants share certain assumptions and knowledge about the subject under discussion. The actors assumed in the various encounters we suggested that their imaginary adversaries knew the reasons for their anger. This made it unnecessary for them to spell out in detail all the circumstances leading up to the confrontations. Abbreviated syntactic forms could be used without fear of being misunderstood. When speaking their monologues, however, the actors could not assume that the experimenter would understand a particular anecdote or opinion unless it were explained, a process that required a full syntactical deployment.

Dialogue is context bound. In the words of Williams (1970), "Language need only add what the context cannot communicate. Fragmented speech under such circumstances is efficient, not incomplete."

Emotion and Verbal Regression

We believe that the simplification of syntax associated with the expression of anger can be understood best as a regression of language performance to earlier and more primitive forms of expression. High frequency of interrogatives, imperatives, and profanities and few expressions of tentativeness have been described as characteristic of the speech of young children (McCarthy, 1930; Loban, 1963; Hunt, 1970). We were able to show in Chapter 3 how verbal behavior acquires greater syntactic complexity and subtlety with age. Of interest to us, in this connection, are results of a study of suicide notes indicating that messages written "under heightened drive" tend to be simple and sterotyped (Osgood & Walker, 1959).

The Facilitating Effect of
Dialogue upon the Expression of Anger

We have noted several times already that the actors appeared to be most angry when engaged in simulated dialogues. Although they were able to become angry when discussing past provocations or strongly-held convictions, their emotional intensity, as judged by the experimenter, did not appear to be as high. The actors confirmed the experimenter's impression, stating that they actually felt most angry when participating in imaginary arguments.

We have assumed that the two volunteers chose confrontations with opponents for their angry segments because of the scenarios suggested to them by the experimenter. It could be argued, however, that the need to display anger, rather than the instructions, influenced the speakers to act out explosive arguments. They perhaps would have created imaginary adversaries to shout at no matter what instructions they were given. We carefully analyzed the content of the male actor's angry samples recorded under uninstructed conditions and found that this was not the case. In only one of six angry samples did he create a scene of confrontation. During the other five angry segments, he spoke about past incidents that had angered him or discussed more general issues about which he had strong, resentful feelings.

Since the most explosive samples of anger we collected were under instructed conditions, it is possible that genuine rage requires the existence of a real or imagined enemy. Can the speaker himself be that enemy? Probably not. We did record a few examples of self-directed verbal attacks during the practice sessions and were not impressed by the degree of anger expressed. In all such cases, the actors reported feeling sad rather than angry, a phenomenon that is congruent with the psychoanalytic view of depression as retroflexed anger.

Real versus Simulated Anger

To what extent can we assume that data derived from simulated angry behavior applies to situations of genuine, spontaneous rage? We already have indicated our reasons for believing that the acted-out emotions of the actors cannot be distinguished from spontaneous feelings. The volunteers themselves reported experiencing the subjective sensations of anger, as predicted by the James-Lange Theory of Emotions. We should add that neither actor was aware of the variables being measured. That they could have consciously manipulated the syntactic and paralinguistic elements from which the categories were constructed appear to us to be extremely remote.

In order to test further the genuineness of the actors' affective display, we compared their scores with those of the angry young man observed in family therapy. Differences between his angry and nonangry samples, as identified by independent judges, were in the same direction as the actors' scores for all categories distinguishing angry from natural segments. This is additional, persuasive evidence that the simulated emotion produced by the actors cannot be distinguished, at least with our measures, from the spontaneously aroused feeling.

Summary

We compared samples of "angry" and "natural" speech, generated by two paid actor-volunteers, and found significant differences in a number of our verbal categories. Under the influence of intense simulated anger, both actors decreased their use of categories reflecting tentativeness and increased their use of immature structures, suggesting a regression to earlier, simpler syntactic forms. The effect of such variables as sex and personality on styles of angry discourse requires additional studies with subjects of various backgrounds.

Notes

1. Because of technical difficulties, only six of the seven sets of speech samples were suitable for transcription and analysis.

Chapter 8
Summary and Conclusions

With this chapter, we have reached the end of our journey. What has been accomplished? What remains to be done?

Summary of Verbal Behavior Studies

Building upon observations gathered in the course of psychoanalytic practice, we brought to the study of verbal behavior certain basic assumptions. It seemed to us that, since much of the knowledge of psychiatric diagnosis and treatment had been acquired through the study of spoken language, a systematic, clinically inspired approach to the analysis of speech, made possible by the development of electronic recording instruments, would be useful. Trained in the psychoanalytic tradition, we were convinced that unconscious psychological conflicts, as well as conflict-free ego and superego structures, are reflected in styles of verbal behavior. Although not underestimating the importance of phonological and semantic aspects of speech, we believed that the choice of syntactic structures was a particularly faithful and measurable reflection of thinking and behavioral styles. Since speech itself is a form of behavior, we felt confident that sampling an individual's spoken language under controlled conditions of stress would lead to clinically useful generalizations about his pattern of psychological defense mechanisms.

The relationship of spoken language to thought is undoubtedly more complicated and less direct than its relationship to nonverbal behavior. According to Vygotsky (1962), words are not simply reflections of thoughts. Thought and speech develop independently, although they obviously intersect very early in life. If words do not mirror thoughts, they probably are subject to similar patterns of organization, so that for a given individual styles of thinking and speech should contain similar although not identical syntactic structures.

We have focused upon psychological defense or coping mechanisms as reflected in verbal behavior. The 14 speech categories we described in Chapter 2 can be scored with adequate interjudge reliability, appear to be related to clinically meaningful thinking and behavior, are used to different degrees by different individuals, and are largely dependent upon syntactic and paralinguistic rather than semantic criteria. The speech variables we used for category construction have a slow rate of change and therefore are suitable for the study of personality traits. All our verbal measures are found in the spontaneous speech of 5-year-old children; therefore, their frequency of occurrence should not be associated strongly with levels of intelligence or educational achievement.

Our method of data collection requires volunteers to speak uninterruptedly for 10 minutes on any subject or subjects that they choose. We have found this nondirective procedure suitable for the gathering of spontaneous speech from normal subjects between the ages of 5 and 85, as well as from a broad range of psychologically deviant adults.

In Chapter 3, we studied the effects of age and sex on the choice of syntactic structures. Our results showed sharp fluctuations in the use of most categories in childhood and early adolescence, followed by a leveling-off in midadolescence and adulthood. We discovered that changes in frequency associated with increasing age are not linear and cannot be explained entirely in terms of cognitive and linguistic development. The data become more meaningful when age-specific shifts in the strength of drives and defenses are taken into account. With respect to sex, consistent differences in several categories exist in most age groups. These differences generally can be associated with sexual variations in nonverbal behavior.

In Chapter 4, we compared a normal control group to six groups of individuals sharing deviant styles of thinking and acting. Significant differences distinguished all deviant populations from the controls in one or more categories. In many instances, syntactic patterns and symptomatic behavior showed striking parallels. In general, our findings were consistent with patterns of psychological defense mechanisms attributed to these deviant groups by psychoanalytically trained clinicians. We found that thematic content and grammatical style appear to be closely associated, suggesting that the interpretation of symptomatic thinking and behavior does not require familiarity with lexical meaning.

We attempted in Chapter 5 to relate styles of speaking to the personality characteristics of individual subjects. Taking advantage of the large amount of spontaneous speech made available by the publication of the Watergate transcripts, we applied our method to spoken-language samples of Nixon, Dean, Haldeman, and Ehrlichman. Comparisons with normal control subjects and groups of delusional, impulsive, depressive, and compulsive patients suggested that the former President may have been clinically depressed during the time the conversations were recorded. We sketched personality profiles of the four Watergate participants by comparing samples of their speech with each other and with the four patient groups. The verbal styles of the conspirators appeared to reflect, in many instances, personality characteristics observed in their public behavior.

Because of the obvious advantages of applying a system of verbal behavior analysis to samples of spontaneous writing, we compared in Chapter 6 segments of free speech and free writing produced by the same individuals. Our results showed that almost all verbal mechanisms used in our system appear with approximately equal frequency in the two modes of expression. Intrasubject comparisons indicated consistency of performance for about half the categories created from syntactic structures. These findings indicate the possible usefulness of our method for the analysis of the free writing found in diaries, letters, suicide notes, and so forth.

Finally, in Chapter 7, we undertook the analysis of an affective state, explosive anger. Four new categories, with a more rapid rate of change, were added to our measures in order to reflect quickly changing behavior. A comparison of "angry" and "natural" speech produced by two paid actors showed significant differences in a number of verbal categories. We found an increased use of immature speech mechanisms under "angry" conditions, suggesting that strong emotions may be associated with a regression of spoken language to more simple syntactic structures.

Applications of our Method

Other researchers have applied part or all of our method to a variety of clinical problems:

1. Ackerman (1966) studied the speech patterns of groups of third and fifth grade children. Although she changed the data-gathering procedure to stimulate verbal production, her results are comparable to our developmental data reported in Chapter 3.

2. Kiesler, Movlthrop, & Todd (1972) used a number of our categories to develop differential theories of psychotherapy and behavior modification.

3. Along more clinical lines, Eichler (1966) applied our method to the speech of sociopathic subjects.

4. We have referred several times to Steinberg's (1973) use of our measures in his analysis of the characters of James Joyce's *Ulysses*.

5. Investigators have used various modifications of our method to study the defenses of depressed patients (Hinchliffe, Lancashire, & Roberts, 1971) and chronic psychiatric patients (Tarlow, Alevizos, & Callahan, 1976). Wherever the procedure has been used as recommended in our publications with groups of subjects comparable to those we have studied, the results have approximated our findings closely.

6. Recently, Natale, Dahlberg, & Jaffe (1978) reported the results of a longitudinal study in which seven of our categories were used to examine the "progressive alteration of defensive language" in seven patients undergoing psychoanalysis. According to the authors, "The magnitude of defensive speech displayed by a patient was able to predict significantly the durations of psychoanalysis undergone in 4 of 7 cases."

Improving our Method

The data generated by our verbal studies strongly suggest that our system can reflect important personality characteristics as well as state-dependent affective changes. It is equally clear, however, that significant personality dimensions escape detection by our method. This is particularly noticeable in the analysis of the Watergate transcripts; a number of well-known characteristics of the participants are not mirrored by frequency of use of our categories.

While we cannot expect of a single method of investigation that it reflect all aspects of thought and behavior, we may be able to broaden the range of applicability of our procedure, as well as sharpen its analytic powers, by (1) developing new categories, (2) changing our present categories, and/or (3) modifying our data-collection procedures.

Developing New Categories

In developing our method, we have created and tested new categories continually. Those we have found to be stable and discriminating have been incorporated into our system; the others we have discarded. As we study new populations or undertake investigations having different goals, the need for additional categories may become obvious. Once developed, we apply them to previously studied groups, thus increasing our interpretive powers.

An example of this process has been the introduction of several personal pronouns into our system. Although not used originally in the analysis of normal and deviant adult speech, their ability to reflect characteristic thinking and behavior became clear when we studied the speech of children and emotionally aroused adults. Once we established their intrasubject reliability, we applied them fruitfully to the study of the original normal and deviant populations.

New measures, perhaps many, will be developed in the future. We are not certain yet which grammatical structures will prove suitable for the creation of new categories; quantifiers and tenses appear to be fertile areas for future investigation.

Changing Present Categories

We believe that we can improve our instrument by modifying certain categories currently in use. An example of a measure we may improve by redefinition is evaluators. As now scored, this category includes expressions of judgment in the areas of morality, propriety, ethics, esthetics, and convenience. Quantifying each of these areas separately may enable us to distinguish reflections of ego, superego, and ego-ideal structures.

Modifying Data-Collection Procedures

The possibilities here are almost endless. Monologues can be compared to dialogues or group discussions, topics can be suggested to volunteers, the time available for speaking can be shortened or lengthened, natural conversations can be studied, diagnostic and therapeutic interviews can be monitored, and so on.

We have been reluctant to modify our procedure so long as personality has been the focus of our attention. The monologue, generated in response to relatively nondirective instructions, provides, in our opinion, the greatest variety of reflections of ego and superego structures. Laffal (1965) has written that free speech "has the greatest variety of contents and the greatest unpredictability of content at any given moment" (p. 95). Narrowing the choice of topics tends to reduce individual variations (Robinson, 1965). Dialogue probably has the same effect, since speakers bring to a conversation certain shared assumptions. Vygotsky (1962) characterized the structurally impoverished speech of dialogue as "abbreviated" compared to the more fully deployed syntax found in the monologue. His notion of abbreviated speech is close to Basil Bernstein's (1959, 1960) concept of restricted linguistic codes. According to Bernstein, dialogue, particularly when carried on by individuals who are well known to each other, favors the use of language characterized by fewer syntactic choices than that found in more elaborate codes. Ego and superego structures are represented more fully in the syntactically developed monologue.

We believe that modifications in our data-collection procedures may prove to be useful in the study of interactional processes where the focus of attention is on state-dependent variables rather than personality traits. We took a modest step in this direction, in Chapter 7, when we asked two actors to convey angry feelings in specific, imaginary situations.

Computerized Collection and Scoring of Verbal Data

It is well known that studies of verbal behavior, even the most elementary, are extremely time consuming. We have found that recording, transcribing, and scoring one 10-minute sample of free speech takes several hours. A content analysis of one complete diagnostic or therapeutic interview is so costly that few investigators have found the venture worthwhile. Procedural rather than conceptual difficulties have blocked the rapid acquisition of knowledge in the field. If it were possible to obtain computer assistance for the recording and processing of speech data, not only would great economies be achieved, but a significant increase in the uniformity of collection and scoring methods would result.

More than 15 years ago, Joseph Jaffe (1962) presented to the Annual Meeting of the Academy of Psychoanalysis an optimistic picture of the future use of computers in verbal behavior research. Describing in considerable detail how a computer might assist an investigator in the transcription, scoring, and analysis of vocal and verbal signals, he predicted that the scientific community would

> shortly see the experimental introduction of a computer as a functioning link in the patient–therapist dyad. Receiving physiological, vocal, and lexical data from both participants, the computer will correlate many variables simultaneously, far beyond the symbolic capacity of the most artful psychoanalyst. The results, produced moments after reception of the data, will be "fed back" to the therapist while the transaction is still in progress. . . . The results are unpredictable, yet may perhaps be as astounding as was the advent of the X-ray and fluoroscope in chest disease.

Obstacles to Computer-Assisted Investigation of Speech

So confident was Jaffe of the imminent, widespread use of computers in psychoanalytic research that he found it necessary to deal at length with the anticipated resistance to the idea from his audience. During the almost 20 years since Jaffe's presentation, technological obstacles have proved to be far more formidable than resistance from the psychoanalytic community.

Two principal difficulties continue to thwart efforts at greater use of computers in verbal behavior research. The first is the problem of automatically transcribing verbal signals from individuals having differences in pronunciation and accent. Some progress has been made, but an accurate, inexpensive method, we can confidently state, will not be developed in the near future. Since the transcription of words is the most time-consuming part of verbal behavior research, studies requiring the analysis of large amounts of speech continue to be unrealistic undertakings. The second difficulty is that content-analysis methods requiring great subtlety of judgment are not suitable for automatic, computerized scoring. No system of verbal-behavior analysis that depends extensively upon inference can be programmed successfully for computer processing (Gottschalk, 1975).

Although Jaffe (1962), during his discussion of computers in psychoanalytic research, considered at length the semantic aspects of speech, he referred hardly at all to syntactic structures, which are far more adaptable to automatic scoring. We find this oversight puzzling, since Jaffe himself did pioneer work in the description of verbal defenses (1960a).

Computerized Scoring of our Categories

Of the 14 trait-dependent categories we are using currently, how many are suitable for automatic scoring? Of those categories not now suitable for electronic scoring, how many can we modify in that direction without significantly decreasing the analytic power of our system? The following five categories already can be scored by a computer, since no knowledge of lexical meaning is required: (1) quantity of speech, (2) *I*, (3) *we*, (4) *me*, and (5) negatives. With minor modifications in scoring procedures, we automatically can score long pauses, rate of speech, qualifiers, retractors, and explainers. The last three measures are dependent upon a relatively small number of commonly used words and phrases, and little will be lost if an occasional expression requiring human judgment is left unscored.

If subdivided into several discrete categories, both evaluators and expressions of feeling should be suitable for computer processing. Programs capable of classifying content of comparable complexity already exist. The task of compiling vocabularies reflecting the most common uses of these categories is a time-consuming but not conceptually formidable challenge. Nonpersonal references cannot be adapted easily to computer scoring because some familiarity with meaning is required. Other strategies for detecting impersonal verbal expression exist, however, and some of these can be used to create automatically scorable categories.

Only one of our categories, direct references, may be lost if we convert to a completely automated system. Since this measure is one of our better verbal reflections of ego functioning, its loss will affect the sensitivity of the instrument. It is possible that we shall be able to compile a vocabulary comprising those words and expressions generally used to refer to the experiment and experimenter, which will permit computerized scoring without significant loss of analytic power.

Transformational Grammar and Verbal Style

Let us consider the following group of sentences:

1. In 1979 the Baltimore Orioles won the American League pennant.

2. The Baltimore Orioles won the American League pennant in 1979.

3. The Baltimore Orioles in 1979 won the American League pennant.

4. The American League pennant was won by the Baltimore Orioles in 1979.

5. The pennant of the American League was won by the Baltimore Orioles in 1979.

6. The Orioles of Baltimore won the American League pennant in 1979.

All of these sentences are grammatically correct and have the same meaning. Transformational grammarians would say that they constitute different surface structures derived from a common deep structure. Every natural language has a set of transformational rules that allow its speakers to say the same thing in different ways. These rules are not creative; that is, they do not introduce new meanings, only new forms.

Although the six sentences are grammatically correct and identical in meaning, they differ profoundly in style. We can place our verbal system within a linguistic framework by stating that we are studying the relationship between behavior and stylistic preferences for certain transformational rules. Patterns of defense mechanisms are reflected by the habitual use of certain transformations. We can illustrate this relationship by assuming that passive individuals preferentially use certain passive rather than active transformational rules. Compared to more active persons, we would expect them to make greater use of sentences like #4 and #5, rather than #1 and #2. In Chapter 4, we showed that inactive or helpless psychiatric patients do have a preference, in fact, for certain passive syntactic structures.

We believe than an analysis of the preferences for transformational rules shown by groups of individuals sharing patterns of deviant behavior may be a fruitful approach to the study of adaptation. To our knowledge, no such attempt has been made, although certain investigators have tried to integrate transformational grammar and psychoanalytic theory in other ways. Edelson (1973), for example, has compared the transformational rules governing the conversion of deep to surface structures to the primary process mechanisms that change latent dream content into manifest dream content. We do not believe Edelson's analogy to be a useful one. Both deep and surface syntactic structures possess all the linguistic characteristics of secondary process operations. As Martindale

(1976) has correctly pointed out, Chomsky's (1957) transformations disappear in regressed psychological states.

Up to this point, we have assumed that syntactic structures, being devoid of meaning, can directly reflect only style, not intent. It was with great interest, therefore, that we read the recent clinical report of Dahl et al. (1978), in which the authors state "that certain syntactic properties of a psychoanalyst's interventions communicate countertransference wishes and other warded-off contents." In one amusing example presented by Dahl et al., an analyst is trying to direct a patient's attention to his negative way of discussing his problems. The analyst is quoted as saying, ". . . this is the way it has always been presented in terms of negatives," rather than, "You have always presented it in terms of negatives." His grammatical elimination of the patient leads Dahl et al. to accuse the analyst of "psychological murder by syntax." We wish to reiterate our conviction that specific desires cannot be identified from meaningless syntactic structures. At most, we may infer the existence of conflict but not the actual content of disguised wishes. To pursue the path indicated by Dahl et al. is to lend encouragement to the kind of wild analysis freely indulged in by psychoanalytic biographers.[1]

As a final example of the clinical application of transformational grammar, we wish to cite the work of Bandler & Grinder (1975), two linguists who have transformed themselves into psychotherapists. Bandler & Grinder recommend as a strategy of psychotherapy the systematic translation of surface structures into deep ones. Impressed by the obvious defensive purposes served by many transformations, they believe that therapists can gain access to repressed and denied material by rigorously reconstructing the meaning and logical relationships (deep structure) of a patient's remark (surface structure). If, for example, a patient says, "People don't like me," the therapist is encouraged to ask, "What people don't like you?" If, on the basis of previous work with the patient, the therapist thinks he knows who the "people" are, he might ask, "Do you mean your parents don't like you?"

We are not sure that Bandler & Grinder actually have discovered anything not already known to experienced psychotherapists. Attacking surface structures in the way they propose is a form of ego analysis that has been practiced widely for many years by therapists of a variety of schools. We suspect that Bandler & Grinder have done little more than pour old wine into new bottles, substituting the metaphors of transformational grammar for those of psychoanalysis.

"Le Style est L'homme Même"*

De Buffon's words, uttered over 200 years ago (1753), remind us that there is nothing new in approaching personality through characteristic behavior. Modern technology enables us to record and preserve various aspects of verbal and nonverbal behavior for microscopic study. Methods for investigating larger units of behavior, however, are less well developed and still depend primarily upon clinical observation.

We must temper our enthusiasm for precise analysis of small segments of behavior with the realization that we easily can miss the forest for the trees. In focusing narrowly upon one channel of communication, as we have done, we run the further risk of developing a fragmented view of human response to stress. We must not forget that we are concerned with only one facet of a complex, psychophysiological process, the integrating principles of which still are largely unknown.

Note

1. The reader may wonder how we can reconcile our belief that style has no meaning with our hopes that the study of grammar can lead to the understanding of intent. Although we do not favor the wild analysis of grammatical structures, we think that it is possible to correlate subjects' themes with their manner of expressing them. Such an analysis can lead to a general association of content and style but never to an interpretation of a specific syntactic structure.

*Style makes the man.

Appendix A
Scored Sample

For readers interested in applying our verbal analysis method to their own research material, we have prepared a scored sample for those categories requiring judgment on the part of the scorer. Of our 14 categories, 6 are scored automatically: number of words, pauses, rate, *I*, *we*, and *me*. We have scored our sample for the other 8 categories. The reader should review the scoring procedure in Chapter 2 before reading the scored sample. The categories have been abbreviated as follows:

Personal References	P
Nonpersonal References	NP
Direct References	DR
Evaluators	Ev
Explainers	Ex
Feelings	F
Qualifiers	Q
Retractors	R
Negatives	N

Figure A-1 Scored Sample of Free Speech.

Well, I'm 21 and I go to the University
     P   P

of Maryland. This is my fourth year in
                NP

college. These two years I have enjoyed
                         P   F

more than the first two years. And I

have been connected more closely with my
        P

field that I had hoped to get into.
                 P

I was a day commuter for the first two
  P

years and lived at home. I financed my
          P   P

own college by working during the summers

and taking that money and applying it to

my college education. And then these two

years have been financed by the Navy pro-
     NP

gram which I am now part of. They have
           P   NP

paid for my complete tuition, and they

paid for my books. In general, this is
NP   NP

190

a   very   good   way   of   financing   my   last
        Ev

two   years   of   school.   I   find   this   is   an
                           NP

interesting   experiment   in   that   we   have   some
      DR   Ex   NP

patients   on   our   wards   taping   for   10   or

15   minutes   during   the   daytime   and   then

writing   diaries   in   the   evening.   It   should
                           NP

be   interesting   in   the   final   study   to   see

what   the   results   are.   I   hope   to   be   able
        NP   P

to   do   this   and   learn   a   little   more

about   the   study   that's   being   carried   on
        DR   NP

here   and   in   the   part   I   am   functioning
                        P

and   the   rest   of   the   student   nurses   are
                        P

functioning   to   contribute   to   it.   This   is
                        NP

my   second   month   in   psychiatry   and   I   have
                        P

enjoyed   my   experience   there   very   much.   It
  F

<u>has been</u> most interesting working with all
  NP

the patients and <u>not</u> only comparing their
            N

reaction <u>but</u> also seeing how <u>I react</u> to
      R   P

them. One of the most interesting examples

<u>we have</u> <u>is</u> one thing <u>I had</u> and <u>who</u>
  NP   NP   P

<u>seems</u> to have many compulsions. And <u>this</u>
P Q

<u>has led</u> to many feelings on part of
  NP

the nursing and medical staff as to how

to handle it. And <u>we were talking</u> about
                    NP

this today and find that <u>everyone is</u>
                         NP

<u>using</u> many different approaches to this.

<u>Many of them seem to be responding</u> or
            NP Q

be affecting him and <u>he is responding</u> to
                    P

them. <u>But</u> <u>it's</u> very interesting to find
      R   NP

out all of the inner feelings of people

who   are   working   with   him   and   how   they
     NP

are   reacting   to   his   behavior   though   I
  NP   R

have   only   had   slight   contact   with   him.
 P

But   in   the   next   week   I   plan   to   have
 R   P

more   contact   with   him   that   would -- since
                                   Ex

that   will   be   my   last   week   on   the   ward.
     NP

And   so   I   can   also   summarize   on   my   own
     Ex   P

feelings   about   this   young   man.   The   month

that   I   have   left   in   Psychiatry   I'll   be
       P   P

spending   out   at   Spring   Grove   Mental   Insti-

tution   and   I   understand   it's   a   complete
                  Q   NP

different   setting   there.   I   am   uncertain   as
                              P

to   my   own   feelings   about   how   I   will
                                    P

accept   only   half   work   with   the   patients

in   that   they   only   have   one   ward   meeting
 Ex   NP

once   a   week.   They rarely get   to   see
                    NP

their   doctors   except   when   absolutely   neces-

sary.   But   then   again   it will allow   us
        R   NP

to   form   new   relationships   to   people   and

possibly   in   some   further   way   not   only   in
Q   N

their   development   and   possible   recovery   but
                                                  R

in   our   own   development   of   personal   rela-

tionships   with   other   people.   I have   many
                                    P

handy   work   types   of   hobbies   of   which   I

am   now   doing   embroidery   of   which   I like
P   P F

to   do   more   of   or   have   more   time   to

do   more   of.   I'd also like   to   have   more
                  P   F

time   to   do   some   of   the   knitting   and

other   things   that   I   do   now.   And   I'm
                                              P

looking   forward   to   graduation   in   June

194

which <u>I think</u> <u>we all are</u> and be able
      Q   NP

to have some time to do more of the

other things that <u>we would like</u> to do
                  NP

in the way of our own hobbies which is

painting and reading -- more along the

novel line than the text-book line. And,

<u>since</u> June is <u>not</u> too far off, <u>we are</u>
Ex   N

<u>all very happy</u> about this. <u>I am anxious</u>
 NP   F   P F

to go home again next week to be able

to see my family and the two <u>lovely</u>
                                Ev

dogs <u>we have</u> there. My <u>father's</u> presently
     P   P

showing one of the dogs and <u>I am anxious</u>
                             P F

to find out whether or <u>not</u> <u>he's won</u> any
                     N   NP

more medals. <u>They are</u> <u>lovely</u> dogs and
               NP   Ev

<u>they're</u> gray and white with black noses
 NP

195

and ears with a pompadour type tail such

as that of a Pomeranian. <u>They only stand</u>
                                           NP

about 18 to 20 inches high <u>but</u> <u>resemble</u>
                                       R   NP

more like a teddy bear. And <u>they're</u> very
                                     NP

<u>lovable</u> dogs. And <u>they're</u> always getting
 Ev   NP

into mischief. And <u>my brother grows</u> by
                              P

leaps and bounds everytime <u>I see</u> him so
                                  P

<u>this will be</u> interesting to see how much
    NP

<u>he's grown</u> this time. And as for my
     P

mother, <u>it will be</u> interesting to see what
           NP

new things <u>she has started</u> at home in
                   P

the way of projects or what local family

news <u>she has gathered</u> to relate to me.
              P

<u>My sister's getting married</u> the end of
                 P

the month. <u>Therefore,</u> <u>I'll be making</u> plans
                Ex   P

with her when <u>I go</u> home as to what
                P

196

to   wear   and   what   arrangements   <u>will   have</u>
                                              NP

<u>to   be   made</u>。   <u>It   will   be</u>   interesting   to
      NP   NP

see   what   arrangements   <u>she's   made</u>   and   what
                                        P

kind   of   a   wedding   <u>she   hopes</u>   to   have
                                    P

and   exactly   what   her   <u>plans   are</u>   on   her
                                       NP

honeymoon。

Table A–1. Conversion of Raw Scores to Final Scores.

Category	Raw Score	Final Score
Quantity of Speech	855 words	855 words
Long Pauses (only pauses over 5 sec.)	8 sec. & 13 sec. (3 + 8)	11 sec.
Rate (# words ÷ nonsilent minutes to the nearest 15 sec.)	855 ÷ 9.75	87.7 wpm
Nonpersonal References $\frac{\text{Nonpersonal ref.} \times 1000}{\text{nonpers. + pers.}}$	Nonpersonal ref. = 41 Personal ref. = 43	488.1

(All other categories are calculated by multiplying the raw score by a corrective figure. The corrective figure is obtained by dividing 1000 by the number of words and rounding off to 3 places after the decimal. Corrective figure for this protocol is 1000 ÷ 855 = 1.170.)

Negatives	4	4.7
Direct References	2	2.3
Evaluators	4	4.7
Explainers	6	7.0
Feelings	7	8.2
Qualifiers	5	5.9
Retractors	7	8.2
I	34	39.8
We	7	8.2
Me	1	1.2

Appendix B
Personality Profiles of Watergate Conspirators

The following personality profiles of the Watergate conspirators were presented to judges who matched them with the sets of verbal scores. When given to the judges, the profiles were not identified by name; rather, they were identified by letter, as shown. The correct name–letter matches are:

Nixon:	Profile *A*	Haldeman:	Profile *C*
Dean:	Profile *B*	Ehrlichman:	Profile *D*

Profile A

A has a tendency to speak in a concrete, personal manner. He is concerned with people known to him and events, rather than abstract ideas. Among the four participants, *A* is the least inhibited in expressing affect. The data suggest not only a generally resistant attitude but also a need to deny unpleasant aspects of reality. *A* has a tendency to reverse himself, possibly a streak of impulsiveness. There is a concern with what is right and wrong or proper and improper. In summary, *A*'s speech is concrete, centered around himself and people known to him; he is able to express affect. He can make decisions but may do so impulsively, and there is a strong tendency to reverse himself. *A* may deny unpleasant aspects of reality and can be moralistic and dogmatic.

Profile B

B's style of speaking is impersonal and abstract. He can express affect, despite a relatively impersonal style. He has a generally positive approach in his relationships with others, as well as an ability to consider and appreciate reality even when it is disagreeable. *B*'s profile suggests an unimpaired ability to make decisions and commitments; he doesn't take back decisions once they are made. There is no evidence of impulsivity or brashness in his speech. *B*'s tendency to reason gives his speech a certain intellectual flavor. He shows relatively great concern about questions of right and wrong, propriety, etc. In summary, *B*'s speech reflects somewhat more of an "intellectual," reasoning tendency than that of the other participants. He has a generally positive approach, can make decisions, shows no signs of impulsivity and can express emotion. He is concerned about questions of morality and propriety.

Profile C

C's speech appears impersonal and mechanical. His profile also indicates a tendency both to place a wall between himself and others and to deny unpleasant reality. *C*'s scores suggest no difficulty in making decisions and commitments. There may be, however, an impulsive streak or, in a more positive sense, an ability to consider a variety of possibilities in a given situation. *C* is more likely to make categorical statements than to give reasons for thoughts and actions. His speech shows no great preoccupation with questions of right and wrong, propriety and impropriety, etc. In summary, *C* emerges as rather impersonal and cold. He is a laconic "no" man who establishes barriers and perhaps denies unpleasant aspects of reality. He can make decisions without hesitation but there is a tendency to reconsider, perhaps a touch of impulsivity. There is little in the way of rationalization. *C* states his point of view dogmatically, without indicating his own emotions about the propriety of such behavior.

Profile D

Although not extremely impersonal, the relative lack of emotion lends a certain mechanical quality to *D*'s speech. He appears to have no difficulty making decisions and sticking to them. There is also little attempt to rationalize behavior. *D* has a tendency toward dogmatic discourse, yet is able to consider all aspects of reality. His profile reveals no excessive preoccupation with questions of morality or propriety.

References

Ackerman, H. Speech patterns of third and fifth grade children. Thesis, University of Maryland, College Park, 1966.

Andreasen, N. J. C., & Pfohl, B. Linguistic analysis of speech in affective disorders. *Archives of General Psychiatry*, 1976, *33*, 1361–1367.

Arieti, S. Manic–depressive psychosis. In S. Arieti (ed.), *American handbook of psychiatry*. New York: Basic Books, 1959.

Aronson, H., & Weintraub, W. Sex differences in verbal behavior related to adjustive mechanisms. *Psychological Reports*, 1967, *21*, 965–971. (a)

Aronson, H., & Weintraub, W. Verbal productivity as a measure of change in affective status. *Psychological Reports*, 1967, *20*, 483–487. (b)

Aronson, H., & Weintraub, W. Personal adaptation as reflected in verbal behavior. In A. W. Siegman & B. Pope (eds.), *Studies in dyadic communication*. New York: Pergamon Press, 1972.

Balkan, E. R., & Masserman, J. H. The language of phantasy: III. The language of the phantasies of patients with conversion hysteria, anxiety state, and obsessive–compulsive neuroses. *The Journal of Psychology*, 1940, *10*, 75–86.

Bandler, R., & Grinder, J. *The structure of magic I: A book about language and therapy*. Palo Alto, Calif.: Science and Behavior Books, 1975.

Becker, T. E. Latency. *Journal of the American Psychoanalytic Association*, 1965, *13*, 584–590.

Benton, A. L.; Hartman, C. H.; & Sarason, I. G. Some relations between speech behavior and anxiety level. *Journal of Abnormal and Social Psychology*, 1955, *51*, 295–297.

Bernstein, B. A public language: Some sociological implications of a linguistic form. *British Journal of Sociology*, 1959, *10*, 311–326.

Bernstein, B. Language and social class. *British Journal of Sociology*, 1960, *11*, 271–276.

Bernstein, B. A sociolinguistic approach to socialization: with some reference to educability. In F. Williams (ed.), *Language and poverty: Perspectives on a theme*. Chicago: Rand McNally, 1970.

Binder, J. Personal communication. September 15, 1975.

Birdwhistell, R. L. Masculinity and femininity on display. In S. Weitz (ed.), *Nonverbal communication*. New York: Oxford University Press, 1974.

Blass, T., & Siegman, A. W. A psycholinguistic comparison of speech, dictation, and writing. *Language and Speech*, 1975, *18*, 20–34.

Blos, P. *On adolescence*. New York: Free Press of Glencoe, 1962.

Blos, P. Preadolescent organization. *Journal of the American Psychoanalytic Association*, 1958, *6*, 47–56.

Boder, D. P. The adjective–verb quotient: A contribution to the psychology of language. *Psychological Record*, 1940, *22*, 310–343.

Bohannon, J. N. III, & Marquis, A. L. Children's control of adult speech. *Child Development*, 1977, *48*, 1002–1008.

Boomer, D. S. Review of *Psycholinguistics: Experiments in spontaneous speech* by F. Goldman-Eisler, *Lingua*, 1970, *25*, 152–164.

Bornstein, B. On latency. *The Psychoanalytic Study of the Child*, 1951, *6*, 279–285.

Brazelton, T. B. The origin of reciprocity. Paper presented to the Department of Psychiatry, University of Maryland, Baltimore, March 1974.

Brown, R., & Fraser, C. The acquisition of syntax. In U. Bellugi & R. Brown (eds.), *The acquisition of language*. Chicago: University of Chicago Press, 1964.

Bruch, H. Psychiatric aspects of obesity in childhood. *The American Journal of Psychiatry*, 1943, *99*, 752–757.

Buck, R. W.; Savin, V. J.; Miller, R. E.; & Caul, W. F. Communication of affect through facial expressions in humans. *Journal of Personality and Social Psychology*, 1972, *23*, 362–371.

Busemann, A. *Die Sprache der Jugend als Ausdruck der Entwicklungsrhythmik*. Jena, Germany: Fisher, 1925.

Cameron, N. The paranoid pseudocommunity. *The American Journal of Sociology*, 1943, *49*, 32–38.

Cameron, N. Paranoid conditions and paranoia. In S. Arieti (ed.), *American handbook of psychiatry*. New York: Basic Books, 1959.

Chafetz, M. E. Addictions. III: Alcoholism. In A. M. Freedman & H. I. Kaplan (eds.), *Comprehensive textbook of psychiatry*. Baltimore: Williams & Wilkins, 1967.

Chomsky, N. *Syntactic structures*. The Hague, Netherlands: Mouton, 1957.

Chomsky, N. Formal discussion of W. Miller & S. Ervin, "The development of grammar in child language." In U. Bellugi & R. Brown (eds.),

The acquisition of language. Chicago: University of Chicago Press, 1964.

Committee on the Judiciary of the House of Representatives. *Submission of recorded presidential conversations by President Richard Nixon*. Washington, D.C.: U.S. Government Printing Office, 1974.

Condon, W. S., & Ogston, W. D. Sound film analysis of normal and pathological behavior patterns. *The Journal of Nervous and Mental Disease*, 1966, *143*, 338–347.

Corrigan, R. A scalogram analysis of the development of the use and comprehension of "because" in children. *Child Development*, 1975, *46*, 195–201.

Coyne, J. C. Depression and the response of others. *Journal of Abnormal Psychology*, 1976, *85:2*, 186–193.

Dahl, H.; Teller, V.; Moss, D.; & Trujillo, M. Countertransference examples of the syntactic expression of warded-off contents. *Psychoanalytic Quarterly*, 1978, *47*, 339–363.

Darwin, C. *The expression of the emotions in man and animals*. (First published in 1872.) New York: Philosophical Library, 1955.

Davis, D., & Taft, R. A measure of preference for speaking rather than writing and its relationship to expressive language skills in adolescents. *Language and Speech*, 1976, *19*, 224–235.

Davis, M. *Understanding body movement: An annotated bibliography*. New York: Arno Press, 1972.

Davitz, J. R., & Davitz, L. J. The communication of feelings by content-free speech. *The Journal of Communication*, 1959, *9*, 6–13.

De Buffon, George Louis Leclerc. *Discourse on his admission to the French Academy*, 1753.

Deutsch, H. *Selected problems of adolescence*. New York: International Universities Press, 1967.

DeVito, J. A. Levels of abstraction in spoken and written language. *Journal of Communication*, 1967, *17*, 354–361.

Dibner, A. S. Cue-counting: A measure of anxiety in interviews. *Journal of Consulting Psychology*, 1956, *20*, 475–478.

Edelheit, H. Speech and psychic structure. The vocal–auditory organization of the ego. *Journal of The American Psychoanalytic Association*, 1969, *17*, 381–412.

Edelson, M. Language and dreams: The interpretation of dreams revisited. In *The Psychoanalytic Study of the Child*, vol. 27. New York: Quadrangle, 1973.

Edelson, M. *Language and interpretation in psychoanalysis*. New Haven and London: Yale University Press, 1975.

Eibl-Eibesfeldt, I. Similarities and differences between cultures. In S.

Weitz (ed.), *Nonverbal communication*. New York: Oxford University Press, 1974.

Eichler, M. The application of verbal behavior analysis to the study of psychological defense mechanisms: Speech patterns associated with sociopathic behavior. *The Journal of Nervous and Mental Disease, 141:6,* 1966, 658–663.

Eisdorfer, C. Psychophysiologic and cognitive studies in the aged. In G. Usdin & C. K. Hofling (eds.), *Aging: The process and the people*. New York: Brunner/Mazel 1978.

Ekman, P., & Friesen, W. V. Nonverbal leakage and clues to deception. *Psychiatry,* 1969, *32,* 88–106.

Erikson, E. *Young man Luther*. New York: Norton, 1958.

Fahey, V. K.; Kamitomo, G. A.; & Cornell, E. H. Heritability in syntactic development: A critique of Munsinger and Douglass. *Child Development,* 1978, *49,* 253–257.

Fairbanks, G., & Hoaglin, L. W. An experimental study of the durational characteristics of the voice during the expression of emotion. *Speech Monographs,* 1941, *8,* 85–90.

Federn, P. *Ego psychology and the psychoses*. New York: Basic Books, 1952.

Feldstein, S. Vocal patterning of emotional expression. In J. H. Masserman (ed.), *Science and psychoanalysis,* vol. 7. New York: Grune & Stratton, 1964.

Fenichel, O. *The psychoanalytic theory of the neuroses*. New York: Norton, 1945.

Fink, M.; Jaffe, J.; & Kahn, R. L. Drug induced changes in interview patterns: Linguistic and neurophysiologic indices. In G. J. Sarwer-Foner (ed.), *The dynamics of psychiatric drug therapy*. Springfield, Ill.: Charles C. Thomas, 1960.

Freedman, D. A. On hearing, oral language, and psychic structure. In R. R. Holt & E. Peterfreund (eds.), *Psychoanalysis and contemporary science,* vol. 1. New York: Macmillan, 1972.

Freud, A. *Normality and pathology in childhood*. New York: International Universities Press, 1965.

Freud, A. On certain difficulties in the preadolescent's relation to his parents. In *The Writings of Anna Freud,* vol. 4. New York: International Universities Press, 1968.

Freud, S. Inhibitions, symptoms, and anxiety. In J. Strachey (ed.), *Standard edition,* vol. 20. London: Hogarth, 1959. (a)

Freud, S. Mourning and melancholia. In E. Jones (ed.), *Collected papers,* vol. 4. New York: Basic Books, 1959. (b)

Freud, S. Psychoanalytic notes on an autobiographical account of a case of paranoia (dementia paranoides). In E. Jones (ed.), *Collected papers*, vol. 3. New York: Basic Books, 1959. (c)

Freud, S. Negation. In J. Strachey (ed.), Standard edition, vol. 19. London: Hogarth, 1961.

Freud, S. The psychopathology of everyday life. In J. Strachey (ed.), Standard edition, vol. 6. London: Hogarth, 1966.

Friedman, J. Weight problems and psychological factors. *Journal of Consulting Psychology*, 1959, *23*, 524–527.

Frosch, J., & Wortis, S. B. A contribution to the nosology of the impulsive disorders. *American Journal of Psychiatry*, 1954, *111*, 132–138.

Gesell, A.; Ilg, F. L.; & Ames, L. B. *Youth: The years from ten to sixteen*. New York: Harper & Row, 1956.

Gleser, G. C.; Gottschalk, L. A.; & John, W. The relationship of sex and intelligence to choice of words: A normative study of verbal behavior. *Journal of Clinical Psychology*, 1959, *15*, 182–191.

Glover, E. Psychoanalysis, a handbook for medical practitioners and students of comparative psychology. London: Staples Press, 1949.

Goldman-Eisler, F. *Psycholinguistics: Experiments in spontaneous speech*. New York: Academic press, 1968.

Goldman-Eisler, F. The predictability of words in context and the length of pauses in speech. *Language and Speech*, 1958, *1*, 226–231.

Gottschalk, L. A. The application of a method of content analysis to psychotherapy research. Paper presented at the meeting of the Society for Psychotherapy Research, Philadelphia, June, 1973.

Gottschalk, L. A. A computerized scoring system for use with content analysis scales. *Comprehensive Psychiatry*, 1975, *16*, 77–90.

Gottschalk, L. A., & Gleser, G. C. An analysis of the verbal content of suicide notes. *British Journal of Medical Psychiatry*, 1960, *33*, 195–204.

Gottschalk, L. A.; Gleser, G. C.; & Hambidge, G. Jr. Verbal behavior analysis: Some content and form variables in speech relevant to personality adjustment. *A.M.A. Archives of Neurology and Psychiatry*, 1957, *77*, 300–311.

Gottschalk, L. A., & Hambidge, G. Jr. Verbal behavior analysis: A systematic approach to the problem of quantifying psychologic processes. *Journal of Projective Techniques*, 1955, *19*, 387–409.

Hall, E. T. *The hidden dimension*. New York: Doubleday, 1966.

Harrell, L. E. Jr. A comparison of the development of oral and written language in school-age children. *Monographs of the Society for Research in Child Development*, 1957, *22* (3, Serial No. 66).

Higgins, G. V. *The friends of Richard Nixon*. Boston: Little, Brown, 1974.

Hinchliffe, M. K.; Lancashire, M.; & Roberts, F. J. Depression: Defense mechanisms in speech. *British Journal of Psychiatry*, 1971, *118*, 471–472.

Hinchliffe, M. K.; Vaughan, P. W.; Hooper, D.; & Roberts, F. J. The melancholy marriage: An inquiry into the interaction of depression. II Expressiveness. *British Journal of Medical Psychology,* 1977, *50,* 125–142.

Horowitz, M. W., & Berkowitz, A. Structural advantage of the mechanism of spoken expression as a factor in differences in spoken and written expression. *Perceptual and Motor Skills,* 1964, *19,* 619–625.

Horowitz, M. W., & Newman, J. B. Spoken and written expression: An experimental analysis. *Journal of Abnormal and Social Psychology,* 1964, *68,* 640–647.

Hunt, K. W. Syntactic maturity in school children and adults. *Monographs of the Society for Research in Child Development,* 1970, *35* (1).

Hutson, B. A., & Shub, J. Developmental study of factors involved in choice of conjunctions. *Child Development,* 1975, *46,* 46–52.

Hymes, D. Open discussion of M. Bullowa, L. G. Jones, & T. G. Bever, "The development from vocal to verbal behavior in children." In U. Bellugi & R. Brown (eds.), *The acquisition of language.* Chicago: University of Chicago Press, 1964.

Jaffe, J. Communication networks in Freud's interview technique. *Psychiatric Quarterly,* 1958, *32,* 456–473.

Jaffe, J. Formal language patterns as defensive operations. In D. A. Barbara (ed.), *Psychological and psychiatric aspects of speech and hearing.* Springfield, Ill.: Charles C. Thomas, 1960. (a)

Jaffe, J. Social factors in the doctor–patient relationship. In J. H. Masserman (ed.), *Science and Psychoanalysis,* vol. 4. New York: Grune & Stratton, 1960. (b)

Jaffe, J. Dyadic analysis of two psychotherapeutic interviews. In L. A. Gottschalk (ed.), *Comparative psycholinguistic analysis of two psychotherapeutic interviews.* New York: International Universities Press, 1961.

Jaffe, J. Electronic computers in psychoanalytic research. Paper presented at the Annual Meeting of The Academy of Psychoanalysis, May 4–6, 1962, Toronto, Canada.

Kahn, R. L., & Fink, M. Changes in language during electroshock therapy. In P. H. Hoch & J. Zubin (eds.), *Psychopathology of communication.* New York: Grune & Stratton, 1958.

Kanfer, F. H. Verbal rate, content, and adjustment ratings in experimentally structured interviews. *The Journal of Abnormal and Social Psychology,* 1959, *58,* 305–311.

Kasl, S. V., & Mahl, G. F. The relationship of disturbances and hesitations in spontaneous speech to anxiety. *Journal of Personality and Social Psychology,* 1965, *1,* 425–433.

Kendon, A. Movement coordination in social interaction: Some examples described. *Acta Psychologica,* 1970, *32,* 101–125.

Kiesler, D. J.; Movlthrop, M. A.; & Todd, T. S. *A psycholinguistic scoring system for the obsessive personality*. Atlanta: Emory University Press, 1972.

Kohen-Raz, R. *The child from 9 to 13*. Chicago: Aldine-Atherton, 1971.

Laffal, J. *Pathological and normal language*. New York: Atherton Press, 1965.

Lalljee, M., & Cook, M. Anxiety and ritualized speech. *British Journal of Psychology*, 1975, *66*, 299–306.

Lees, R. Formal discussion of R. Brown, C. Fraser, and U. Bellugi, "Explorations in grammar evaluation." In U. Bellugi & R. Brown (eds.), *The acquisition of language*. Chicago: University of Chicago Press, 1964.

Lenneberg, E. H. Speech as a motor skill with special reference to nonaphasic disorders. In U. Bellugi & R. Brown (eds.), *The acquisition of language*. Chicago: University of Chicago Press, 1964.

Lewis, M. Language, cognitive development, and personality. *Journal of American Academy of Child Psychiatry*, 1977, *16*, 646–661.

Lifton, R. J. On psychohistory. In R. R. Holt & E. Peterfreund (eds.), *Psychoanalysis and contemporary science*, vol. 1. New York: Macmillan, 1972.

Loban, W. B. The language of elementary school children. *National Council of Teachers of English Research Report, No. 1*, 1963.

Lorenz, M. Language as expressive behavior. *Archives of Neurology and Psychiatry*, 1953, *70*, 277–285.

Lorenz, M. Expressive behavior and language patterns. *Psychiatry*, 1955, *18*, 353–366.

Lorenz, M., & Cobb, S. Language behavior in manic patients. *Archives of Neurology and Psychiatry*, 1952, *67*, 763–770.

Lorenz, M., & Cobb, S. Language behavior in psychoneurotic patients. *Archives of Neurology and Psychiatry*, 1953, *69*, 684–694.

Lorenz, M., & Cobb, S. Language patterns in psychotic and psychoneurotic subjects. *Archives of Neurology and Psychiatry*, 1954, *72*, 665–673.

Maher, B. The language of schizophrenia: A review and interpretation. *British Journal of Psychiatry*, 1972, *120*, 3–17.

Mahl, G. F. Disturbances and silences in the patient's speech in psychotherapy. *The Journal of Abnormal and Social Psychology*, 1956, *53*, 1–15.

Mahl, G. F. The lexical and linguistic levels in the expression of the emotions. In P. H. Knapp (ed.), *Expression of the emotions in man*. New York: International Universities Press, 1963.

Mahl, G. F. Some observations about research on vocal behavior. In D. M.

Rioch and E. A. Weinstein (eds.), *Disorders of Communication*, Baltimore: Williams and Willkins, 1964.

Martindale, C. The grammar of altered states of consciousness: A semiotic reinterpretation of aspects of psychoanalytic theory. In D. P. Spence (ed.), *Psychoanalysis and contemporary science*, vol. 4. New York: International Universities Press, 1976.

McCarthy, D. *The language development of the preschool child*. Minneapolis: University of Minnesota Press, 1930.

McCarthy, D. Some possible explanations of sex differences in language development and disorders. *The Journal of Psychology*, 1953, 35, 155–160.

McGuire, M. T., & Lorch, S. A model for the study of dyadic communication. *The Journal of Nervous and Mental Disease*, 1968, *146*, 221–229.

Menyuk, P. *Sentences children use*. Cambridge, Mass: M.I.T. Press, 1969.

Meyer, B. C. Some reflections on the contribution of psychoanalysis to biography. In R. R. Holt & E. Peterfreund (eds.), *Psychoanalysis and contemporary science*, vol. 1. New York: Macmillan, 1972.

Michaels, J. J. *Disorders of character*. Springfield, Ill.: Charles C. Thomas, 1955.

Michaels, J. J. Character structure and character disorders. In S. Arieti (ed.), *American Handbook of Psychiatry*. New York: Basic Books, 1959.

Milmoe, S.; Novey, M. S.; Kagan, J.; & Rosenthal, R. The mother's voice: Postdictor of aspects of her baby's behavior. *Proceedings of the 76th Annual Convention of the American Psychological Association*, 1968, 3, 463–464.

Milmoe, S.; Rosenthal, R.; Blane, H. T.; Chafetz, M. E.; & Wolf, I. The doctor's voice: Postdictor of successful referral of alcoholic patients. *Journal of Abnormal Psychology*, 1967, 72, 78–84.

Mirin, B. The formal aspects of schizophrenic verbal communication. *Genetic Psychological Monographs*, 1955, 52, 150–190.

Monroe, R. R. *Episodic behavioral disorders*. Cambridge, Mass: Harvard University Press, 1970.

Moskowitz, B. A. The acquisition of language. *Scientific American*, Nov. 1978, 239:5, 92–108.

Munsinger, H. A reply to Fahey, Kamitomo, & Cornell. *Child Development*, 1978, 49, 258–259.

Munsinger, H., & Douglass, A. The syntactic abilities of identical twins, fraternal twins, and their siblings. *Child Development*, 1976, 47, 40–50.

Murray, D. C. Talk, silence and anxiety. *Psychological Bulletin*, 1971, 75, 244–260.

Natale, M. Effects of induced elation–depression on speech in the initial interview. *Journal of Consulting and Clinical Psychology*, 1977, 45, 45–52.

Natale, M.; Dahlberg, C. C.; & Jaffe, J. The relationship of defensive language behavior in patient monologues to the course of psychoanalysis. *Journal of Clinical Psychology*, 1978, 34, 466–470.

Nelson, K. First steps in language acquisition. *Journal of American Academy of Child Psychiatry*, 1977, 16, 563–583. (a)

Nelson, K. E. Aspects of language acquisition and use from age 2 to age 20. *Journal of American Academy of Child Psychiatry*, 1977, 16, 584–607. (b)

Nelson, W. M. III, & Groman, W. D. Neurotic verbalizations: An exploration of a gestalt therapy assumption. *Journal of Clinical Psychology*, 1975, 31, 732–737.

Nemiah, J. C. Psychoneurotic disorders: II. Obsessive–compulsive and neurotic depressive reactions. In A. M. Freedman & H. I. Kaplan (eds.), *Comprehensive Textbook of Psychiatry*. Baltimore: Williams and Wilkins, 1967.

Newman, S., & Mather, V. G. Analysis of spoken language of patients with affective disorders. *The American Journal of Psychiatry*, 1938, 94, 913–942.

O'Connell, R. C.; Griffen, W. J.; & Norris, R. C. Syntax of kindergarten and elementary school children: A transformational analysis. *National Council of Teachers of English Research Report No. 8*, 1967.

O'Dell, J. W., & Winder, P. Evaluation of a content-analysis system for therapeutic interviews. *Journal of Clinical Psychology*, 1975, 31, 737–744.

Olim, E. G. Maternal language styles and cognitive development. In F. Williams (ed.), *Language and poverty: Perspectives on a theme*. Chicago: Rand McNally, 1970.

Osgood, C. E., & Walker, E. G. Motivation and language behavior: A content analysis of suicide notes. *The Journal of Abnormal and Social Psychology*, 1959, 59, 58–67.

Osser, H. Biological and social factors in language development. In F. Williams (ed.), *Language and poverty: Perspectives on a theme*. Chicago: Rand McNally, 1970.

Palermo, D. S., & Molfese, D. L. Language acquisition from age five onward. *Psychological Bulletin*, 1972, 78, 409–428.

Piaget, J. *The language and thought of the child*, 3rd ed. London: Routledge and Kegan Paul, 1959.

Poole, M. E., & Field, T. W. A comparison of oral and written code elaboration. *Language and Speech*, 1976, *19*, 305–312.

Pope, B., & Siegman, A. W. The effect of therapist verbal activity level and specificity on patient productivity and speech disturbance in the initial interview. *Journal of Consulting Psychology*, 1962, *26*, 489.

Pope, B., & Siegman, A. W. Interviewer specificity and topical focus in relation to interviewee productivity. *Journal of Verbal Learning and Verbal Behavior*, 1965, *4*, 188–192.

Rado, S. The problem of melancholia. *International Journal of Psychoanalysis*, 1928, *9*, 420–438.

Rapaport, D. *Organization and pathology of thought*. New York: Columbia University Press, 1951.

Rascovsky, A.; de Rascovsky, M. W.; & Schlossberg, T. Basic psychic structure of the obese. *International Journal of Psychoanalysis*, 1950, *31*, 144–149.

Rather, D., & Gates, G. P. *The palace guard*. New York: Harper & Row, 1974.

Ricoeur, P. *Freud and philosophy*. New Haven: Yale University Press, 1970.

Robinson, W. P. The elaborated code in working class language. *Language and Speech*, 1965, *8*, 243–252.

Ruesch, J., & Prestwood, A. R. Anxiety: Its initiation, communication, and interpersonal management. *Archives of Neurology and Psychiatry*, 1949, *62*, 527–550.

Ryle, G. *The concept of mind*. New York: Barnes and Noble, 1965.

Samovar, L., & Sanders, F. Language patterns of the prostitute: Some insights into a deviant subculture. *et cetera*, 1978, *35*, 30–36.

Sapir, E. Speech as a personality trait. *American Journal of Sociology*, 1927, *32*, 892–905.

Schachter, S., & Singer, J. E. Cognitive, social, and physiological determinants of emotional state. *Psychological Review*, 1962, *69*, 379–399.

Schafer, R. *A new language for psychoanalysis*. New Haven: Yale University Press, 1976.

Scheflen, A. E. Quasi-courtship behavior in psychotherapy. *Psychiatry*, 1965, *28*, 245–257.

Scherer, K. R. Acoustic concomitants of emotional dimensions: Judging affect from synthesized tone sequences. In S. Weitz (ed.), *Nonverbal communication*. New York: Oxford University Press, 1974.

Schick, A. Psychosomatic aspects of obesity. *Psychoanalytic Review*, 1947, *34*, 173–183.

Schneidman, E. S. Suicide notes reconsidered. *Psychiatry*, 1973, *36*, 379–394.

Shope, G. L.; Hedrick, T. E.; & Green, R. G. Physical/verbal aggression: Sex differences in style. *Journal of Personality*, 1978, *46*, 23–41.

Siegel, S. *Non-parametric statistics for the behavioral sciences*. New York: McGraw-Hill, 1956.

Siegman, A. W. The meaning of silent pauses in the initial interview. *The Journal of Nervous and Mental Disease*, 1978, *166*, 642–654.

Siegman, A. W., & Pope, B. Effects of question specificity and anxiety-producing messages on verbal fluency in the initial interview. *Journal of Personality and Social Psychology*, 1965, *2*, 522–530.

Sommer, R. Studies in personal space. *Sociometry*, 1959, *22*, 247–260.

Sommer, R. Further studies of small group ecology. *Sociometry*, 1965, *28*, 337–348.

Sommer, R. Sociofugal space. *American Journal of Sociology*, 1967, *72*, 654–660.

Spence, D. P. Tracing a thought stream by computer. In B. B. Rubinstein (ed.), *Psychoanalysis and contemporary science*, vol. 2. New York: Macmillan, 1973.

Starkweather, J. A. Content-free speech as a source of information about the speaker. *Journal of Abnormal and Social Psychology*, 1956, *52*, 394–402.

Steinberg, E. *Stream of consciousness and beyond in Ulysses*. Pittsburgh: University of Pittsburgh Press, 1973.

Steingart, I., & Freedman, N. A language construction approach for the examination of self/object representation in varying clinical states. In R. R. Holt & E. Peterfreund (eds.), *Psychoanalysis and contemporary science*, vol. 1. New York: Macmillan, 1972.

Steingart, I., & Freedman, N. The organization of body-focused kinesic behavior and language construction in schizophrenic and depressed states. In D. P. Spence (ed.), *Psychoanalysis and contemporary science*, vol. 4. New York: International Universities Press, 1976.

Stunkard, A. J. Eating patterns and obesity. *Psychiatric Quarterly*, 1959, *33*, 284–295.

Tarlow, G.; Alevizos, P. N.; & Callahan, E. J. Assessing the conversational behavior of psychiatric patients: Reliability and validity of the Verbal Report Form (VRF). *Canadian Journal of Behavioral Science*, 1976, *8:4*, 334–346.

Tucker, G. J., & Rosenberg, S. D. Computer content analysis of schizophrenic speech: A preliminary report. *American Journal of Psychiatry*, 1975, *132*, 611–616.

Tuckman, J.; Kleiner, R. J.; & Lavell, M. Emotional content of suicide notes. *American Journal of Psychiatry*, 1959, *116*, 59–63.

Vernon, M., & Miller, W. G. Language and nonverbal communication in cognitive and affective processes. In B. B. Rubinstein (ed.), *Psychoanalysis and contemporary science*, vol. 2. New York: Macmillan, 1973.

Vygotsky, L. S. *Thought and language*. Cambridge, Mass.: M.I.T. Press, 1962.

Waelder, R. The structure of paranoid ideas. A critical survey of various theories. *International Journal of Psychoanalysis*, 1951, *32*, 167–177.

Watson, O. M. Conflicts and directions in proxemic research. *Journal of Communication*, 1972, *22*, 443–459.

Weintraub, W., & Aronson, H. The application of verbal behavior analysis to the study of psychological defense mechanisms: Methodology and preliminary report. *Journal of Nervous and Mental Disease*, 1962, *134*, 169–181.

Weintraub, W., & Aronson, H. The application of verbal behavior analysis to the study of psychological defense mechanisms, II: Speech pattern associated with impulsive behavior. *Journal of Nervous and Mental Disease*, 1964, *139*, 75–82.

Weintraub, W., & Aronson, H. The application of verbal behavior analysis to the study of psychological defense mechanisms, III: Speech pattern associated with delusional behavior. *Journal of Nervous and Mental Disease*, 1965, *141*, 172–179.

Weintraub, W., & Aronson, H. The application of verbal behavior analysis to the study of psychological defense mechanisms, IV: Speech pattern associated with depressive behavior. *Journal of Nervous and Mental Disease*, 1967, *144*, 22–28.

Weintraub, W., & Aronson, H. Application of verbal behavior analysis to the study of psychological defense mechanisms, V: Speech pattern associated with overeating. *Archives of General Psychiatry*, 1969, *21*, 739–744.

Weintraub, W., & Aronson, H. Verbal behavior analysis and psychological defense mechanisms, VI: Speech pattern associated with compulsive behavior. *Archives of General Psychiatry*, 1974, *30*, 297–300.

Weitz, S. (ed.), *Nonverbal communication*. New York: Oxford University Press, 1974.

Werkman, S. L., & Greenberg, E. S. Personality and interest patterns in obese adolescent girls. *Psychosomatic Medicine*, 1967, *29*, 72–80.

Williams, F. Language, attitude, and social change. In F. Williams (ed.), *Language and poverty*. Chicago: Rand McNally, 1970.

Zuckerman, M.; Lubin, B.; Vogel, L.; & Valerius, E. Measurement of experimentally induced affects. *Journal of Consulting Psychology*, 1964, *28*, 418–425.

Index